50 Ways for a Startup to Make Money From Chatgpt

David Murray-Hundley

Published by The Grumpy Entrepreneur, 2023.

50 WAYS FOR A STARTUP TO MAKE MONEY FROM CHATGPT

First edition. May 9, 2023.

Copyright © 2023 David Murray-Hundley.

ISBN: 979-8223712459

Written by David Murray-Hundley.

To my team, my rocks, Trina, Harriet and Georgina

To my mates Kevin and Jan who annoy me with countless AI
youtube videos

50 ways for a startup to make money from ChatGPT

Author: David Murray-Hundley

Who is David Murray-Hundley "The Grumpy Entrepreneur"

British based although in my 20s spent far to much time in the US and partying in Monaco.

Worked on many web firsts but during the dotcom boom I got to be a founding part of Commerce One which was a Dotcom darling.

I then went bust, Commerce One went chapter 11 and I was 30. But when you have slept in bus shelters at the age of 18, you take everything in your stride.

Since then have built numerous companies, messed some up and have Pario Ventures which is me and my mates business with over 100 investments.

Why am I called The Grumpy Entrepreneur, we have my wife to thank for that. Her idea back in 2012 and since then I have trademarked it. Anyway enough of me, lets move on.

Feel free to drop me a message.

Twitter @thegrumpye

Linkedin - David Murray-Hundley The Grumpy Entrepreneur | LinkedIn[1]

Website - ParioVentures.com

www.thegrumpyentrepreneur.co.uk

---

1.   https://www.linkedin.com/in/thegrumpyentrepreneur/

1. Introduction

Each of these chapters will delve into the different ways startups can make money using ChatGPT. The book will explain the concepts, the necessary tools, and the potential business opportunities that arise from leveraging ChatGPT's capabilities. Additionally, it will provide real-life examples and case studies of successful startups that have implemented these strategies, along with tips and advice on how to effectively utilize ChatGPT in various industries.

Why did I do this? To be honest I was spending some down time looking at the power of AI in 2023 and my good friends Jan Stanley-Brown and Kevin Doyle who kept sending me Whatsapp messages about how amazing ChatGPT is! Thanks gents. So I will not sit here and say this was months of work. It was me exploring how powerful this stuff is all going to become.

So excuse the formating, the dryness but hopefully some of these ideas might trigger someone to be the next Elon Musk or Reid Hoffman.

Chapter 2: Subscription-Based Services

In this chapter, we will explore how startups can create subscription-based services using ChatGPT. Subscription-based services involve charging customers a recurring fee for access to a product or service, providing a steady stream of revenue for businesses.

1. Develop a ChatGPT-powered tool or service: Identify a need or gap in the market that can be filled by leveraging ChatGPT's capabilities. For instance, you could develop a chatbot that offers expert advice in a specific niche, or an AI-driven content generation tool for businesses and individuals.

2. Implement a tiered subscription model: Offer different subscription plans that cater to various customer needs and budgets. You can have a basic plan with limited features or usage, and more advanced plans with additional features, higher usage limits, or faster response times.

3. Freemium model: Attract users to your service by offering a free version with limited capabilities, and encourage them to upgrade to a paid plan for full access to features and benefits. This model can help you build a user base and generate interest in your service.

4. Integrate ChatGPT with other services: You can enhance the value of your subscription offering by integrating ChatGPT with other tools and services. For example, you could combine ChatGPT with a project management tool or CRM system to provide AI-powered suggestions and insights.

5. Provide personalized experiences: Use ChatGPT's ability to understand context and generate human-like responses to create personalized experiences for your subscribers. You could offer individualized content recommendations, learning materials, or support based on each user's preferences

and needs.

6. Offer exclusive content: In addition to the core ChatGPT-powered service, you could provide subscribers with exclusive content, such as tutorials, webinars, or articles, to enhance the value of their subscription.

7. Implement a referral program: Encourage subscribers to refer friends and colleagues to your service by offering incentives, such as discounts or free months of subscription. This can help you grow your user base and increase revenue.

8. Continuously improve your offering: Regularly gather feedback from your subscribers and monitor usage patterns to identify areas of improvement. Update and expand your service based on user feedback and emerging trends to ensure that it remains valuable and relevant to your subscribers.

9. Market and promote your subscription service: Use content marketing, social media advertising, and targeted marketing campaigns to attract potential subscribers. Share testimonials and case studies from satisfied customers to demonstrate the value and benefits of your ChatGPT-powered subscription service.

By following these steps, startups can create, market, and grow successful subscription-based services using ChatGPT. The key is to identify a unique application for ChatGPT that addresses a market need, and to continuously improve the service based on user feedback and emerging trends.

Chapter 3: Advertising and Sponsored Content

In this chapter, we will explore how startups can use ChatGPT for advertising and sponsored content creation. Advertising and sponsored content are effective ways to promote a brand, product, or service to a targeted audience. By leveraging ChatGPT's natural language processing capabilities, startups can create engaging and personalized ad campaigns and sponsored content that resonate with their target market.

1. Ad copy generation: Use ChatGPT to generate compelling and creative ad copy for various advertising channels, such as social media, search engine marketing, display ads, and native advertising. By inputting relevant keywords, target audience information, and product features, ChatGPT can generate ad copy that captures the attention of potential customers.
2. Personalized ad campaigns: Utilize ChatGPT's ability to understand context and user preferences to create personalized ad campaigns tailored to specific audience segments. This can lead to higher engagement and conversion rates, as the ads will be more relevant and appealing to the target audience.
3. Sponsored content creation: ChatGPT can be employed to create high-quality sponsored articles or blog posts that seamlessly blend with the editorial content on a publisher's website. The AI-generated content will be engaging, informative, and relevant to the target audience, while subtly promoting the brand or product.
4. Social media content: Leverage ChatGPT to create engaging social media posts that promote your brand or products. The

AI can generate a variety of content formats, such as text, captions, and hashtags, to capture the attention of users across different platforms.

5. Influencer collaborations: Use ChatGPT to identify potential influencers in your niche and generate personalized outreach messages. The AI can also help create tailored promotional content for influencers to share with their audience, increasing your brand's visibility and credibility.

6. Email marketing campaigns: ChatGPT can assist in crafting persuasive and personalized email marketing campaigns that drive customer engagement and conversions. The AI can generate subject lines, email body content, and calls-to-action that resonate with the target audience.

7. A/B testing: Utilize ChatGPT to generate multiple variations of ad copy, headlines, and content for A/B testing. This allows you to identify the most effective messaging and design elements for your advertising and sponsored content campaigns.

8. Performance analysis and optimization: ChatGPT can analyze the performance of your advertising and sponsored content campaigns to identify areas for improvement. By incorporating feedback from this analysis, the AI can generate new content or ad variations that yield better results.

By leveraging ChatGPT for advertising and sponsored content creation, startups can effectively promote their brand, products, or services while saving time and resources. The AI's ability to generate engaging and personalized content can lead to higher engagement, conversions, and ROI for your marketing efforts.

Chapter 4: ChatGPT-Powered Customer Support

In this chapter, we will explore how startups can use ChatGPT to enhance their customer support operations. By leveraging ChatGPT's natural language processing and understanding capabilities, startups can provide fast, accurate, and personalized support to their customers, resulting in increased satisfaction and loyalty.

1. Develop a ChatGPT-powered chatbot: Create a chatbot that integrates ChatGPT to handle customer inquiries, providing instant and accurate responses. By training the chatbot with company-specific information and frequently asked questions, it can become a valuable resource for addressing customer concerns and providing support.
2. Multi-channel support: Implement your ChatGPT-powered chatbot across various support channels, such as your website, mobile app, social media platforms, and messaging apps, to provide a consistent support experience for your customers regardless of the platform they choose.
3. Personalized customer interactions: Utilize ChatGPT's contextual understanding to deliver personalized support experiences. The chatbot can remember previous interactions with a customer, allowing it to provide tailored responses and solutions based on their individual needs and preferences.
4. Triage and escalation: Program your ChatGPT-powered chatbot to recognize when an issue requires escalation to a human support agent. By efficiently handling simpler queries, the chatbot can free up your support team's time, allowing them to focus on more complex issues and deliver a higher

level of service.

5. Automate routine tasks: Use ChatGPT to automate routine tasks within the customer support process, such as updating customer information, processing refunds, or sending follow-up messages. This can reduce response times and improve overall customer satisfaction.

6. 24/7 support availability: A ChatGPT-powered chatbot can provide round-the-clock support, ensuring that customers receive assistance whenever they need it. This can be particularly valuable for startups with customers in different time zones or those that have limited resources for staffing a 24/7 support team.

7. Multilingual support: Leverage ChatGPT's language capabilities to provide support in multiple languages, expanding your startup's reach and accommodating a diverse customer base.

8. Feedback collection and analysis: Use your ChatGPT-powered chatbot to collect customer feedback on support interactions and overall product or service experience. Analyze this feedback to identify areas for improvement and enhance your support offerings.

9. Continuous improvement: Train your ChatGPT-powered chatbot with new information and updates regularly, ensuring that it stays up-to-date with your startup's products, services, and policies. Monitor its performance and make adjustments as needed to improve its accuracy and effectiveness.

By implementing ChatGPT-powered customer support, startups can provide efficient, accurate, and personalized assistance to their customers. This can lead to increased customer satisfaction and loyalty, which are essential for the growth and success of any startup.

Chapter 5: Personalized Content Generation

In this chapter, we will explore how startups can use ChatGPT to generate personalized content for their target audience. Personalized content can drive higher engagement, improve customer satisfaction, and strengthen brand loyalty. By leveraging ChatGPT's natural language processing and understanding capabilities, startups can create tailored content that resonates with their audience and helps them stand out in a competitive market.

1. Audience segmentation: Identify and segment your target audience based on demographics, interests, preferences, and behaviors. This information will help you tailor content to address the specific needs and desires of each segment, making it more engaging and relevant.

2. Dynamic content generation: Use ChatGPT to create dynamic content that adapts to individual user preferences and browsing history. This can include personalized product recommendations, news articles, blog posts, or social media updates, which can lead to increased engagement and conversions.

3. Personalized email campaigns: Leverage ChatGPT to craft personalized email marketing campaigns that resonate with your subscribers. By generating subject lines, email body content, and calls-to-action tailored to individual preferences, you can improve open rates, click-through rates, and conversions.

4. AI-driven content curation: Utilize ChatGPT's understanding of context and user preferences to curate content from various sources that match the interests of your

audience. This can help you provide value to your users while also reducing the time and effort required for manual content curation.

5. Personalized learning experiences: For startups in the education and training sector, ChatGPT can be used to create personalized learning materials and assessments that cater to individual learning styles, knowledge levels, and goals.

6. Tailored website experiences: Integrate ChatGPT into your website to generate personalized content and navigation experiences for visitors. By adapting the content and layout based on individual user preferences and behavior, you can increase engagement and conversions.

7. Social media personalization: Use ChatGPT to generate personalized social media content and responses that engage with your audience on a personal level. This can help you build stronger connections with your followers and encourage brand loyalty.

8. ChatGPT-powered content analytics: Analyze user engagement with your personalized content using ChatGPT's AI-driven analytics capabilities. Identify patterns and trends that can inform future content personalization strategies, ensuring that your content remains relevant and engaging.

9. Continuous improvement: Regularly gather feedback from your audience and monitor engagement metrics to identify areas for improvement in your content personalization efforts. Update and refine your ChatGPT-generated content based on this feedback to keep it fresh and engaging.

By incorporating ChatGPT into your content generation strategy, startups can create personalized content that resonates with their target audience and drives higher engagement. This can help startups differentiate themselves in a crowded market, build stronger relationships with their customers, and ultimately, achieve greater success.

Chapter 6: Online Education and Training

In this chapter, we will explore how startups can leverage ChatGPT to enhance their online education and training offerings. By utilizing ChatGPT's natural language processing and understanding capabilities, startups can create personalized, engaging, and efficient learning experiences for their users.

1. AI-driven course creation: Use ChatGPT to generate course content, such as lesson plans, learning objectives, quizzes, and assessments. By inputting relevant keywords, subject matter, and learning goals, ChatGPT can produce high-quality educational content that caters to different learning styles and needs.

2. Personalized learning paths: Leverage ChatGPT to create personalized learning paths for individual students based on their goals, learning pace, and knowledge gaps. This can lead to more efficient and effective learning experiences, as students can focus on the material most relevant to their needs.

3. Tutoring and mentoring: Develop a ChatGPT-powered chatbot that provides tutoring and mentoring services to students. The chatbot can answer questions, provide explanations, and guide students through difficult concepts, offering real-time support and feedback.

4. Peer-to-peer learning: Use ChatGPT to facilitate peer-to-peer learning by connecting students with similar interests, goals, or knowledge levels. The AI can help generate discussion prompts, suggest collaborative activities, and moderate group interactions to ensure a positive and productive learning environment.

5. Language learning: Leverage ChatGPT's multilingual

capabilities to create immersive language learning experiences. The AI can generate language exercises, conversational scenarios, and cultural context, allowing students to practice their language skills in a realistic and engaging way.

6. Adaptive assessments: Employ ChatGPT to create adaptive assessments that adjust the difficulty and content of questions based on individual student performance. This can help identify knowledge gaps and provide a more accurate measure of student progress.

7. Gamification: Utilize ChatGPT to gamify the learning experience by creating engaging and interactive educational games. This can make the learning process more enjoyable and motivate students to stay engaged with the course material.

8. Student engagement and motivation: Use ChatGPT to monitor student engagement and performance, providing personalized feedback and encouragement to keep students motivated and on track. The AI can also identify and address potential barriers to learning, such as lack of understanding or waning interest.

9. Teacher support: Leverage ChatGPT to assist teachers in creating lesson plans, generating teaching materials, and providing personalized support to students. This can help teachers save time and improve the overall effectiveness of their instruction.

10. Continuous improvement: Collect feedback from students and teachers to identify areas for improvement in your online education and training offerings. Regularly update and refine your ChatGPT-generated content based on this feedback to ensure it remains relevant, engaging, and effective.

By incorporating ChatGPT into their online education and training offerings, startups can create personalized, engaging, and efficient learning experiences that cater to the diverse needs of their users. This can help startups differentiate themselves in the competitive online education market, attract more students, and drive better learning outcomes.

Chapter 7: Market Research and Data Analysis

In this chapter, we will explore how startups can use ChatGPT to enhance their market research and data analysis efforts. By leveraging ChatGPT's natural language processing and understanding capabilities, startups can gain valuable insights into their target market, competitors, and industry trends, helping them make informed decisions and drive business growth.

1. Competitor analysis: Utilize ChatGPT to analyze competitors' online presence, marketing strategies, product offerings, and customer reviews. The AI can help identify strengths, weaknesses, opportunities, and threats, enabling startups to make strategic decisions based on competitive landscape insights.

2. Sentiment analysis: Use ChatGPT to perform sentiment analysis on social media posts, customer reviews, and other user-generated content. This can help startups gauge customer opinions and identify areas for improvement in their products, services, or marketing efforts.

3. Trend identification: Leverage ChatGPT to identify emerging trends and patterns in your industry, market, or target audience. By staying ahead of the curve, startups can seize new opportunities and adapt their strategies to capitalize on these trends.

4. Customer segmentation: Employ ChatGPT to analyze customer data and create detailed customer profiles based on demographics, interests, preferences, and behaviors. This information can help startups tailor their marketing and product strategies to better serve their target audience.

5. Survey design and analysis: Use ChatGPT to generate survey questions and analyze the results to gain insights into customer preferences, needs, and opinions. This information can inform product development, marketing strategies, and overall business direction.

6. AI-driven data visualization: Leverage ChatGPT's capabilities to create data visualizations that help communicate complex data and insights in a clear, concise, and visually appealing manner. These visualizations can be used in presentations, reports, and marketing materials to support decision-making and showcase your startup's expertise.

7. Predictive analytics: Utilize ChatGPT to develop predictive models that forecast future trends, customer behaviors, or market changes. These predictions can help startups anticipate potential challenges and opportunities, allowing them to make proactive decisions and stay ahead of the competition.

8. Content analysis: Employ ChatGPT to analyze your startup's own content, identifying patterns and trends that can inform your content strategy. By understanding what types of content resonate with your audience, you can create more engaging and effective marketing materials.

9. Social listening: Use ChatGPT to monitor social media conversations and online discussions related to your industry, brand, or competitors. This can help startups identify potential issues, opportunities, and customer needs, allowing them to respond promptly and effectively.

10. Continuous learning and improvement: Regularly update your ChatGPT-generated market research and data analysis based on new information, trends, or user feedback. This iterative approach can help your startup stay agile and adapt

quickly to changing market conditions.

By incorporating ChatGPT into their market research and data analysis efforts, startups can gain valuable insights that inform strategic decision-making and drive business growth. This can help startups stand out in a competitive market, better serve their customers, and achieve long-term success.

Chapter 8: Enhancing Recruitment and Talent Acquisition

In this chapter, we will explore how startups can leverage ChatGPT to improve their recruitment and talent acquisition processes. By utilizing ChatGPT's natural language processing and understanding capabilities, startups can streamline their hiring process, identify the best candidates, and create a more efficient and effective talent acquisition strategy.

1. Job description generation: Use ChatGPT to generate compelling and accurate job descriptions based on inputted keywords, role requirements, and desired qualifications. This can help attract the right candidates and set clear expectations for the position.
2. Candidate sourcing: Leverage ChatGPT to search through online platforms, such as social media, job boards, and professional networking sites, to identify potential candidates who match your startup's requirements and culture.
3. Candidate screening: Employ ChatGPT to analyze candidate resumes, cover letters, and online profiles, quickly identifying the most relevant and qualified applicants. This can save your startup time and resources by narrowing down the applicant pool early in the hiring process.
4. Interview question generation: Utilize ChatGPT to create customized interview questions that focus on the specific skills, qualifications, and experiences relevant to the role. This can help you gain deeper insights into each candidate's abilities and potential fit with your startup.
5. Automated interview scheduling: Integrate ChatGPT with your recruitment software to automate interview scheduling,

reducing the time and effort required to coordinate between candidates and hiring managers.

6. Candidate communication: Use ChatGPT to draft personalized and engaging messages to candidates throughout the recruitment process. This can help maintain candidate interest and build a positive impression of your startup's employer brand.

7. AI-powered assessments: Leverage ChatGPT to develop customized assessments that evaluate candidates' skills, knowledge, and cultural fit. By incorporating AI-generated scenarios and questions, you can create a more engaging and accurate assessment experience.

8. Reference checking: Employ ChatGPT to automate the reference checking process, reaching out to provided references and collecting relevant information about candidates' past performance, skills, and work habits.

9. Onboarding support: Utilize ChatGPT to create personalized onboarding materials and support resources for new hires. This can help ensure a smooth transition into the company and set the foundation for long-term success and employee satisfaction.

10. Continuous improvement: Regularly gather feedback from hiring managers, candidates, and new hires to identify areas for improvement in your recruitment and talent acquisition process. Incorporate this feedback to refine your ChatGPT-generated resources and strategies, ensuring they remain effective and efficient.

By incorporating ChatGPT into their recruitment and talent acquisition processes, startups can streamline their hiring efforts, identify top candidates, and create a more efficient and effective talent acquisition strategy. This can help startups build a strong team of talented professionals, which is crucial for long-term success and growth.

Chapter 9: Enhancing Product Development and Innovation

In this chapter, we will explore how startups can leverage ChatGPT to boost their product development and innovation efforts. By utilizing ChatGPT's natural language processing and understanding capabilities, startups can generate new ideas, validate concepts, and optimize product features, leading to more successful and competitive products.

1. Idea generation: Use ChatGPT to generate new product ideas or innovative features based on inputted keywords, market trends, or customer needs. This can help startups think outside the box and identify potential opportunities for growth and differentiation.

2. Concept validation: Leverage ChatGPT to validate product concepts by analyzing market data, customer feedback, and competitor offerings. This can help startups determine the viability of their ideas and make informed decisions about which concepts to pursue.

3. Feature optimization: Utilize ChatGPT to analyze user feedback, reviews, and usage data to identify areas for improvement in your product's features and functionality. The AI can help you prioritize updates and enhancements based on customer needs and preferences.

4. Prototyping and design: Employ ChatGPT to generate design specifications, user interface layouts, and user experience concepts for your product. This can help you create more user-friendly and visually appealing products that resonate with your target audience.

5. User testing: Use ChatGPT to create user testing scenarios,

questions, and tasks that evaluate the usability, functionality, and appeal of your product. This can help you identify and address any issues before your product hits the market.

6. Market positioning: Leverage ChatGPT to analyze market trends, customer preferences, and competitor strategies to determine the optimal positioning for your product. This can help you create a compelling value proposition and stand out in a competitive market.

7. Product documentation: Utilize ChatGPT to create comprehensive and user-friendly product documentation, including user manuals, FAQs, and help articles. This can help ensure that customers have the information they need to make the most of your product.

8. Content creation: Employ ChatGPT to generate marketing materials, blog posts, and social media content that highlights your product's features, benefits, and unique selling points. This can help you effectively communicate your product's value to potential customers.

9. Continuous improvement: Regularly gather feedback from customers, partners, and internal stakeholders to identify areas for improvement in your product development and innovation efforts. Incorporate this feedback to refine your ChatGPT-generated resources and strategies, ensuring they remain effective and efficient.

Chapter 10: Streamlining Internal Communication and Collaboration

In this chapter, we will explore how startups can use ChatGPT to improve their internal communication and collaboration efforts. By leveraging ChatGPT's natural language processing and understanding capabilities, startups can create more efficient, organized, and inclusive work environments.

1. Meeting facilitation: Utilize ChatGPT to generate meeting agendas, discussion prompts, and follow-up tasks, helping to keep meetings focused and productive. The AI can also help facilitate virtual meetings by providing real-time transcription and summarization.

2. Task management: Leverage ChatGPT to create, assign, and track tasks within your team or organization. The AI can help prioritize tasks, set deadlines, and ensure that everyone is on the same page regarding expectations and responsibilities.

3. Knowledge sharing: Use ChatGPT to create a centralized knowledge base that stores and organizes important company information, documents, and resources. This can help employees quickly find the information they need and promote knowledge sharing across the organization.

4. Team collaboration: Employ ChatGPT to facilitate collaboration among team members by generating project plans, brainstorming prompts, and communication templates. This can help teams work together more effectively and efficiently.

5. Language translation: Utilize ChatGPT's multilingual capabilities to translate internal communications and resources, allowing

Chapter 10: Enhancing Internal Communication and Team Collaboration

In this chapter, we will explore how startups can leverage ChatGPT to improve their internal communication and team collaboration processes. By utilizing ChatGPT's natural language processing and understanding capabilities, startups can foster a more effective, organized, and transparent work environment.

1. Meeting management: Use ChatGPT to generate meeting agendas, discussion topics, and action items, helping to ensure that meetings are productive and goal-oriented. The AI can also assist in providing real-time transcription and summarization of key points raised during virtual meetings.

2. Task delegation and tracking: Leverage ChatGPT to create, assign, and monitor tasks within your team or organization. The AI can assist in prioritizing tasks, setting deadlines, and maintaining clear communication regarding expectations and responsibilities.

3. Centralized knowledge repository: Employ ChatGPT to develop a comprehensive knowledge base that houses and organizes crucial company information, documents, and resources. This enables employees to quickly access the information they need and promotes a culture of knowledge sharing across the organization.

4. Collaborative project management: Utilize ChatGPT to facilitate collaboration among team members by generating project plans, brainstorming ideas, and creating communication templates. This fosters a more efficient and effective team dynamic, resulting in better overall project outcomes.

5. Language translation and support: Leverage ChatGPT's multilingual capabilities to translate internal communications and resources, allowing employees from different linguistic backgrounds to collaborate seamlessly and feel included within the organization.

6. Training and development: Use ChatGPT to create personalized training materials, workshops, and resources for employees to enhance their skills and knowledge. This helps to ensure continuous professional development and growth within the organization.

7. Conflict resolution: Employ ChatGPT to generate impartial and unbiased solutions to conflicts and disagreements within the team. The AI can provide suggestions for resolving issues in a fair and equitable manner, promoting a harmonious work environment.

8. Decision-making support: Utilize ChatGPT to analyze data, weigh pros and cons, and present well-informed recommendations for various business decisions. This can help teams make more accurate and strategic decisions, leading to better overall performance.

9. Team building and engagement: Leverage ChatGPT to create engaging team-building activities, icebreakers, and morale-boosting initiatives. This fosters a sense of camaraderie and connection among team members, contributing to a positive work culture.

10. Continuous improvement: Regularly gather feedback from employees, managers, and stakeholders to identify areas for improvement in your internal communication and collaboration processes. Use this feedback to refine and optimize your ChatGPT-generated resources and strategies, ensuring that they continue to support your organization's goals and values.

By incorporating ChatGPT into their internal communication and team collaboration processes, startups can create a more effective, organized, and transparent work environment. This helps foster a strong company culture, promotes employee satisfaction, and ultimately contributes to the success and growth of the startup.

Chapter 11: Customer Support and Service Enhancement

In this chapter, we will explore how startups can leverage ChatGPT to improve their customer support and service efforts. By utilizing ChatGPT's natural language processing and understanding capabilities, startups can provide prompt, accurate, and personalized support, enhancing the overall customer experience and building lasting relationships.

1. AI-powered chatbots: Utilize ChatGPT to develop intelligent chatbots that can handle customer inquiries, troubleshoot issues, and provide relevant information. These chatbots can reduce response times, decrease support costs, and provide 24/7 assistance, increasing customer satisfaction.

2. Email support automation: Leverage ChatGPT to automate the generation and categorization of email responses, enabling faster and more accurate replies to customer inquiries. This can help to ensure customers receive timely and appropriate support.

3. Personalized customer interactions: Use ChatGPT to create personalized responses and interactions with customers, taking into account their preferences, previous interactions, and purchase history. This can help make customers feel valued and foster long-term loyalty.

4. Knowledge base development: Employ ChatGPT to create and maintain a comprehensive knowledge base of frequently asked questions, troubleshooting guides, and other support resources. This enables customers to easily find the information they need and reduces the workload on your support team.

5. Social media support: Utilize ChatGPT to monitor and respond to customer inquiries and feedback on social media platforms. This can help your startup provide quick and efficient support, address customer concerns, and showcase your commitment to customer satisfaction.
6. Call center support: Leverage ChatGPT to assist call center agents with real-time information retrieval, script generation, and problem-solving suggestions. This can help agents provide more accurate and efficient support, leading to higher customer satisfaction.
7. Customer feedback analysis: Use ChatGPT to analyze customer feedback, reviews, and survey responses, identifying patterns and trends that can inform your support strategy and overall business direction.
8. Training and development: Employ ChatGPT to create customized training materials and resources for your customer support team, ensuring they have the skills and knowledge necessary to provide excellent support.
9. Quality assurance: Utilize ChatGPT to monitor and evaluate customer support interactions, identifying areas for improvement and ensuring consistent quality across all support channels.
10. Continuous improvement: Regularly gather feedback from customers, support team members, and stakeholders to identify areas for improvement in your customer support and service efforts. Incorporate this feedback to refine your ChatGPT-generated resources and strategies, ensuring they continue to meet the evolving needs of your customers and your organization.

By incorporating ChatGPT into their customer support and service efforts, startups can provide prompt, accurate, and personalized support, enhancing the overall customer experience and building lasting relationships. This not only helps to retain existing customers but also attracts new ones, contributing to the long-term success and growth of the startup.

Chapter 12: Content Creation and Marketing Strategies

In this chapter, we will explore how startups can leverage ChatGPT to optimize their content creation and marketing strategies. By utilizing ChatGPT's natural language processing and understanding capabilities, startups can generate high-quality, engaging, and targeted content that effectively communicates their value proposition and attracts new customers.

1. Blog post generation: Utilize ChatGPT to generate informative and engaging blog posts on topics relevant to your industry, products, or services. This can help establish your startup as an authority in your field and drive organic traffic to your website.

2. Social media content: Leverage ChatGPT to create captivating social media posts, updates, and captions that resonate with your target audience. This can help grow your social media following, increase brand awareness, and generate new leads.

3. Email marketing: Use ChatGPT to craft personalized and targeted email campaigns, including newsletters, promotional offers, and product updates. This can help you maintain ongoing communication with your customers and nurture leads through the sales funnel.

4. Press releases and announcements: Employ ChatGPT to generate professional and newsworthy press releases and announcements for your startup's latest product launches, partnerships, or milestones. This can help you generate media coverage and reach a wider audience.

5. Video scripts: Utilize ChatGPT to create compelling video

scripts for promotional, educational, or informational content. This can help you produce engaging video content that appeals to your target audience and promotes your startup's products or services.

6. Case studies and testimonials: Leverage ChatGPT to develop convincing case studies and testimonials that showcase the success and benefits of your products or services. This can help build trust with potential customers and provide social proof to support your marketing claims.

7. SEO optimization: Use ChatGPT to generate keyword-optimized content that adheres to best practices for search engine optimization. This can help improve your search engine rankings, drive organic traffic, and increase visibility for your startup online.

8. Content curation: Employ ChatGPT to curate relevant and valuable content from around the web, such as industry news, articles, or resources, to share with your audience. This can help you establish your startup as a thought leader and provide value to your target audience.

9. Influencer outreach: Utilize ChatGPT to create personalized outreach messages for potential industry influencers and partners. This can help you establish valuable connections and promote your startup through influencer marketing and collaborations.

10. Continuous improvement: Regularly gather feedback from your audience, customers, and stakeholders to identify areas for improvement in your content creation and marketing efforts. Use this feedback to refine your ChatGPT-generated resources and strategies, ensuring that they continue to support your startup's growth and goals.

By incorporating ChatGPT into their content creation and marketing strategies, startups can generate high-quality, engaging, and targeted content that effectively communicates their value proposition and attracts new customers. This can help startups build brand awareness, generate leads, and drive long-term growth and success.

Chapter 13: Enhancing Recruitment and Talent Management

In this chapter, we will explore how startups can leverage ChatGPT to optimize their recruitment and talent management processes. By utilizing ChatGPT's natural language processing and understanding capabilities, startups can identify, attract, and retain top talent, contributing to a skilled and motivated workforce.

1. Job description generation: Utilize ChatGPT to create clear, concise, and compelling job descriptions that effectively communicate the required skills, responsibilities, and expectations for each role. This can help you attract better-suited candidates and streamline the hiring process.

2. Resume screening: Leverage ChatGPT to automate the screening of resumes and cover letters, identifying the most relevant and qualified candidates for each role. This can save time, reduce human bias, and ensure a more efficient recruitment process.

3. Interview question generation: Use ChatGPT to generate insightful and relevant interview questions tailored to each candidate and role. This can help you better assess the skills, experience, and cultural fit of potential hires.

4. Onboarding materials: Employ ChatGPT to create personalized and engaging onboarding materials, including training resources, company policies, and welcome messages. This can help new hires feel supported and informed as they join your startup.

5. Performance evaluation: Utilize ChatGPT to generate objective and data-driven performance evaluations, identifying areas of strength and opportunities for

improvement. This can help you provide constructive feedback and support employee growth and development.

6. Career development planning: Leverage ChatGPT to create customized career development plans for employees, outlining potential growth opportunities, training resources, and long-term goals. This can help you retain top talent and foster a culture of continuous learning and development.

7. Employee engagement: Use ChatGPT to generate engaging team-building activities, icebreakers, and morale-boosting initiatives. This fosters a sense of camaraderie and connection among team members, contributing to a positive work culture.

8. Internal communication: Employ ChatGPT to facilitate effective communication among team members and departments, generating project updates, meeting agendas, and other important communications. This can help maintain transparency and collaboration within your startup.

9. Talent pool management: Utilize ChatGPT to maintain an organized talent pool, categorizing potential candidates by their skills, experience, and fit for future roles. This can help you quickly identify and recruit top talent as your startup grows.

10. Continuous improvement: Regularly gather feedback from employees, managers, and stakeholders to identify areas for improvement in your recruitment and talent management processes. Use this feedback to refine your ChatGPT-generated resources and strategies, ensuring that they continue to support your startup's growth and goals.

By incorporating ChatGPT into their recruitment and talent management processes, startups can identify, attract, and retain top talent, contributing to a skilled and motivated workforce. This helps create a strong foundation for long-term success and growth, positioning the startup for continued innovation and achievement.

Chapter 14: Streamlining Operations and Workflow Automation

In this chapter, we will explore how startups can leverage ChatGPT to optimize their operations and automate workflows. By utilizing ChatGPT's natural language processing and understanding capabilities, startups can increase efficiency, reduce human error, and focus on higher-value tasks, fostering a more agile and scalable organization.

1. Process documentation: Utilize ChatGPT to generate comprehensive and easy-to-understand process documentation, outlining the necessary steps, responsibilities, and guidelines for various operational tasks. This can help ensure consistency and reduce errors in your startup's day-to-day operations.

2. Task automation: Leverage ChatGPT to identify repetitive and time-consuming tasks that can be automated, and develop scripts or integrations to streamline these tasks. This can help free up valuable time for your team to focus on more strategic and creative tasks.

3. Project management: Use ChatGPT to create project plans, timelines, and task lists, ensuring that your team stays on track and meets deadlines. The AI can also assist in monitoring project progress and generating status reports, helping you maintain transparency and accountability.

4. Inventory management: Employ ChatGPT to develop an intelligent inventory management system that tracks stock levels, predicts demand, and generates reorder alerts. This can help optimize your startup's supply chain and reduce excess inventory costs.

5. Data analysis and reporting: Utilize ChatGPT to analyze complex data sets, identify patterns and trends, and generate actionable insights that inform your business decisions. The AI can also create visually appealing reports and dashboards, helping you effectively communicate your findings to stakeholders.

6. Customer relationship management (CRM) integration: Leverage ChatGPT to enhance your CRM system by automating data entry, generating personalized customer interactions, and providing real-time insights into customer behavior. This can help you better understand and serve your customers, leading to increased loyalty and sales.

7. Quality control: Use ChatGPT to establish quality control measures and protocols, automating the inspection and monitoring of your startup's products or services. This can help you maintain a high standard of quality and reduce the likelihood of defects or customer dissatisfaction.

8. Employee scheduling: Employ ChatGPT to generate fair and efficient employee schedules, taking into account factors such as availability, workload, and skill set. This can help ensure that your team remains productive and motivated, while also minimizing burnout and turnover.

9. Expense tracking and budgeting: Utilize ChatGPT to develop a robust expense tracking and budgeting system, helping you monitor spending, identify areas for cost reduction, and allocate resources effectively. This can contribute to the financial stability and growth of your startup.

10. Continuous improvement: Regularly gather feedback from employees, managers, and stakeholders to identify areas for improvement in your operations and workflow automation efforts. Use this feedback to refine your ChatGPT-generated

resources and strategies, ensuring that they continue to support your startup's growth and goals.

By incorporating ChatGPT into their operations and workflow automation processes, startups can increase efficiency, reduce human error, and focus on higher-value tasks, fostering a more agile and scalable organization. This not only helps startups maintain a competitive edge but also contributes to their long-term success and growth.

Chapter 15: Enhancing Decision-Making and Strategic Planning

In this chapter, we will explore how startups can leverage ChatGPT to improve decision-making and strategic planning processes. By utilizing ChatGPT's natural language processing and understanding capabilities, startups can gain valuable insights, identify opportunities and risks, and make more informed decisions, positioning themselves for long-term success and growth.

1. Market research and analysis: Utilize ChatGPT to gather and analyze market data, including industry trends, competitive landscape, and customer preferences. This can help you identify opportunities and threats, enabling you to make more informed decisions regarding your startup's products, services, and overall direction.

2. Risk assessment: Leverage ChatGPT to conduct a comprehensive risk assessment, identifying potential risks and developing mitigation strategies. This can help you proactively address potential issues and minimize their impact on your startup's operations and growth.

3. Financial forecasting: Use ChatGPT to generate data-driven financial projections, estimating future revenue, expenses, and cash flow. This can help you make better-informed decisions regarding resource allocation, investment, and growth strategies.

4. Scenario planning: Employ ChatGPT to develop and analyze various scenarios, assessing the potential outcomes and impacts of different strategies and decisions. This can help you anticipate future challenges and opportunities, enabling you to make more informed choices.

5. SWOT analysis: Utilize ChatGPT to conduct a SWOT analysis (Strengths, Weaknesses, Opportunities, and Threats) for your startup. This can help you gain a comprehensive understanding of your startup's current position and inform your strategic planning efforts.

6. Goal setting and prioritization: Leverage ChatGPT to establish SMART (Specific, Measurable, Achievable, Relevant, and Time-bound) goals and prioritize them based on their potential impact and feasibility. This can help ensure that your startup remains focused on its most critical objectives.

7. Collaboration and brainstorming: Use ChatGPT to facilitate collaborative brainstorming sessions, generating new ideas and solutions for your startup's challenges and opportunities. The AI can help synthesize diverse perspectives and provide objective insights, enhancing the overall decision-making process.

8. Stakeholder engagement: Employ ChatGPT to communicate effectively with stakeholders, including investors, partners, and customers, ensuring their input and concerns are taken into account in your decision-making and strategic planning processes.

9. Performance tracking and analysis: Utilize ChatGPT to monitor your startup's progress toward its goals, analyzing performance data and identifying areas for improvement. This can help ensure that your startup stays on track and adapts its strategies as needed.

10. Continuous improvement: Regularly gather feedback from employees, managers, and stakeholders to identify areas for improvement in your decision-making and strategic planning processes. Use this feedback to refine your ChatGPT-generated resources and strategies, ensuring that they

continue to support your startup's growth and goals.

By incorporating ChatGPT into their decision-making and strategic planning processes, startups can gain valuable insights, identify opportunities and risks, and make more informed decisions. This positions startups for long-term success and growth, enabling them to adapt and thrive in an ever-evolving business landscape.

Chapter 16: Enhancing Customer Support and Engagement

In this chapter, we will explore how startups can leverage ChatGPT to optimize their customer support and engagement efforts. By utilizing ChatGPT's natural language processing and understanding capabilities, startups can provide more personalized, efficient, and satisfying experiences for their customers, leading to increased loyalty and brand advocacy.

1. AI-powered chatbots: Utilize ChatGPT to create AI-powered chatbots that can assist your customers with inquiries, troubleshooting, and other support needs. This can help reduce response times, improve customer satisfaction, and free up your support team to focus on more complex issues.

2. Social media monitoring and engagement: Leverage ChatGPT to monitor social media channels for customer questions, feedback, and sentiment. The AI can help you identify and address customer concerns proactively, fostering a positive brand reputation and driving customer loyalty.

3. Personalized recommendations: Use ChatGPT to generate personalized product or service recommendations based on your customers' preferences, browsing history, and purchase behavior. This can help increase customer satisfaction, drive repeat business, and boost revenue.

4. Proactive support: Employ ChatGPT to identify common customer pain points and proactively address them through targeted content, resources, or support initiatives. This can help reduce customer frustration and demonstrate your commitment to their success.

5. Customer feedback analysis: Utilize ChatGPT to analyze customer feedback, including reviews, surveys, and social media comments. This can help you identify trends, uncover areas for improvement, and make data-driven decisions to enhance your customer experience.

6. Content personalization: Leverage ChatGPT to create personalized content tailored to each customer's unique needs, preferences, and interests. This can help boost engagement, drive conversions, and foster long-term customer relationships.

7. Multilingual support: Use ChatGPT to provide customer support and resources in multiple languages, catering to a global audience and ensuring that your customers feel valued and understood.

8. Community management: Employ ChatGPT to facilitate and moderate online community discussions, fostering a positive and supportive environment for your customers to connect, share experiences, and seek assistance.

9. Loyalty programs and incentives: Utilize ChatGPT to develop and manage loyalty programs and incentives that reward your customers for their ongoing support and engagement. This can help increase customer retention and drive repeat business.

10. Continuous improvement: Regularly gather feedback from customers, employees, and stakeholders to identify areas for improvement in your customer support and engagement efforts. Use this feedback to refine your ChatGPT-generated resources and strategies, ensuring that they continue to support your startup's growth and goals.

By incorporating ChatGPT into their customer support and engagement efforts, startups can provide more personalized, efficient, and satisfying experiences for their customers. This leads to increased loyalty and brand advocacy, helping startups build a strong foundation for long-term success and growth.

Chapter 17: Strengthening Content Marketing and Copywriting

In this chapter, we will explore how startups can leverage ChatGPT to optimize their content marketing and copywriting efforts. By utilizing ChatGPT's natural language processing and understanding capabilities, startups can create high-quality, engaging, and persuasive content that drives brand awareness, customer engagement, and conversions.

1. Blog post creation: Utilize ChatGPT to generate well-researched, informative, and engaging blog posts on topics relevant to your target audience. This can help establish your startup as an industry authority, drive organic traffic, and nurture leads.

2. Social media content: Leverage ChatGPT to create compelling and shareable social media content that resonates with your audience, fostering engagement, brand awareness, and loyalty.

3. Email marketing: Use ChatGPT to craft personalized and persuasive email campaigns, including newsletters, promotions, and lifecycle emails. This can help improve open rates, click-through rates, and conversions.

4. Landing page copy: Employ ChatGPT to write persuasive and conversion-focused landing page copy that effectively communicates your startup's unique value proposition and drives visitors to take action.

5. Video scripts: Utilize ChatGPT to create engaging and informative video scripts, enhancing your multimedia content marketing efforts and capturing the attention of your audience.

6. Case studies and testimonials: Leverage ChatGPT to craft compelling case studies and testimonials that showcase the success and value of your products or services, building trust and credibility with potential customers.

7. SEO optimization: Use ChatGPT to optimize your content for search engines, including the integration of relevant keywords, metadata, and linking strategies. This can help improve your search engine rankings and drive organic traffic to your website.

8. Content repurposing: Employ ChatGPT to repurpose existing content into different formats or for different channels, maximizing your content's reach and value while saving time and resources.

9. Content strategy development: Utilize ChatGPT to develop a comprehensive content strategy that outlines your startup's goals, target audience, content pillars, distribution channels, and success metrics. This can help ensure that your content marketing efforts are aligned with your startup's objectives and focused on driving results.

10. Continuous improvement: Regularly gather feedback from your audience, employees, and stakeholders to identify areas for improvement in your content marketing and copywriting efforts. Use this feedback to refine your ChatGPT-generated resources and strategies, ensuring that they continue to support your startup's growth and goals.

By incorporating ChatGPT into their content marketing and copywriting efforts, startups can create high-quality, engaging, and persuasive content that drives brand awareness, customer engagement, and conversions. This not only helps startups differentiate themselves from the competition but also lays the foundation for long-term success and growth.

Chapter 18: Optimizing Recruitment and Talent Management

I n this chapter, we will explore how startups can leverage ChatGPT to streamline their recruitment and talent management efforts. By utilizing ChatGPT's natural language processing and understanding capabilities, startups can attract, retain, and develop top talent, ensuring a high-performing and motivated workforce that drives their success and growth.

1. Job description creation: Utilize ChatGPT to create detailed and engaging job descriptions that effectively communicate your startup's requirements, expectations, and company culture. This can help attract the right candidates and reduce the time spent on screening and interviewing.

2. Candidate sourcing: Leverage ChatGPT to develop targeted recruitment strategies, identifying relevant job boards, online communities, and social media channels where potential candidates can be found. This can help increase the quality and quantity of your applicant pool.

3. Resume and cover letter screening: Use ChatGPT to automate the initial screening of resumes and cover letters, identifying candidates that meet your startup's requirements and saving your HR team valuable time and resources.

4. Interview scheduling and coordination: Employ ChatGPT to manage the interview scheduling process, ensuring that candidates, interviewers, and meeting rooms are coordinated effectively and reducing the likelihood of scheduling conflicts.

5. Interview question generation: Utilize ChatGPT to generate relevant and insightful interview questions tailored to each

candidate's skills, experience, and potential fit with your startup's culture. This can help improve the overall quality of your interviews and the insights gained from them.

6. Onboarding and training: Leverage ChatGPT to create personalized onboarding and training materials, ensuring that new hires feel welcomed, supported, and equipped for success in their roles.

7. Performance management: Use ChatGPT to develop data-driven performance management processes, including goal setting, progress tracking, and feedback collection. This can help ensure that your employees remain motivated, engaged, and focused on their professional growth and development.

8. Employee engagement and retention: Employ ChatGPT to identify opportunities for improving employee engagement and retention, such as offering professional development opportunities, creating a positive work environment, and recognizing and rewarding employees for their contributions.

9. Succession planning: Utilize ChatGPT to create a robust succession planning process, identifying high-potential employees, evaluating their readiness for leadership roles, and developing tailored development plans to prepare them for future opportunities.

10. Continuous improvement: Regularly gather feedback from employees, managers, and stakeholders to identify areas for improvement in your recruitment and talent management efforts. Use this feedback to refine your ChatGPT-generated resources and strategies, ensuring that they continue to support your startup's growth and goals.

By incorporating ChatGPT into their recruitment and talent management efforts, startups can attract, retain, and develop top talent, ensuring a high-performing and motivated workforce that drives their success and growth. This not only helps startups maintain a competitive edge but also contributes to their long-term sustainability and success.

Chapter 19: Streamlining Project Management and Collaboration

In this chapter, we will explore how startups can leverage ChatGPT to improve project management and collaboration across their teams. By utilizing ChatGPT's natural language processing and understanding capabilities, startups can enhance communication, increase efficiency, and foster a culture of innovation and teamwork, leading to better project outcomes and long-term success.

1. Project planning and scoping: Utilize ChatGPT to generate detailed project plans, including scope, objectives, tasks, deadlines, and resources. This can help ensure that all stakeholders have a clear understanding of the project requirements and expectations, minimizing the risk of scope creep and delays.

2. Task prioritization and delegation: Leverage ChatGPT to help prioritize tasks based on their impact, urgency, and feasibility. This can help your team members focus on the most important tasks first and ensure that resources are allocated effectively.

3. Meeting agendas and minutes: Use ChatGPT to create and distribute meeting agendas and minutes, ensuring that all team members are informed and aligned on project progress, decisions, and next steps.

4. Knowledge sharing and documentation: Employ ChatGPT to facilitate knowledge sharing and documentation across your teams, capturing best practices, lessons learned, and process improvements. This can help foster a culture of continuous improvement and innovation within your startup.

5. Team communication and collaboration: Utilize ChatGPT to enhance communication and collaboration among team members, generating discussion prompts, brainstorming ideas, and providing feedback. This can help foster a more inclusive and supportive work environment, leading to better project outcomes and increased employee satisfaction.

6. Risk management and mitigation: Leverage ChatGPT to identify potential risks and develop risk mitigation strategies, helping to proactively address potential issues and minimize their impact on your project's success.

7. Progress tracking and reporting: Use ChatGPT to generate project progress reports and dashboards, ensuring that stakeholders remain informed and aligned on project progress and performance.

8. Resource management: Employ ChatGPT to optimize resource allocation, helping to ensure that team members have the necessary tools, support, and capacity to complete their tasks effectively and efficiently.

9. Change management: Utilize ChatGPT to develop and implement change management strategies, ensuring that your team members are prepared and supported as they adapt to new processes, technologies, and ways of working.

10. Continuous improvement: Regularly gather feedback from your team members, managers, and stakeholders to identify areas for improvement in your project management and collaboration efforts. Use this feedback to refine your ChatGPT-generated resources and strategies, ensuring that they continue to support your startup's growth and goals.

By incorporating ChatGPT into their project management and collaboration efforts, startups can enhance communication, increase efficiency, and foster a culture of innovation and teamwork. This not only leads to better project outcomes but also contributes to the long-term success and growth of the startup.

Chapter 20: Boosting Sales and Customer Acquisition

In this chapter, we will explore how startups can leverage ChatGPT to improve their sales and customer acquisition efforts. By utilizing ChatGPT's natural language processing and understanding capabilities, startups can create more targeted, persuasive, and personalized sales strategies that resonate with their audience and drive conversions.

1. Lead generation: Utilize ChatGPT to develop targeted lead generation strategies, identifying and reaching out to potential customers through personalized outreach, content marketing, and social media engagement.

2. Sales script development: Leverage ChatGPT to create persuasive sales scripts tailored to your startup's unique value proposition, target audience, and sales objectives. This can help your sales team communicate more effectively with prospects and convert more leads into customers.

3. Follow-up communication: Use ChatGPT to craft personalized and timely follow-up communications that keep your startup top-of-mind for prospects, nurturing them through the sales funnel and increasing the likelihood of conversion.

4. Sales presentation creation: Employ ChatGPT to generate compelling and informative sales presentations that effectively showcase your startup's products, services, and value proposition, helping to persuade prospects and close deals.

5. Objection handling: Utilize ChatGPT to develop a comprehensive objection handling strategy, equipping your

sales team with the knowledge and resources they need to address common customer concerns and objections confidently.

6. Competitive analysis: Leverage ChatGPT to conduct competitive analysis, identifying your startup's key differentiators and positioning your products or services more effectively in the market.

7. Sales team training: Use ChatGPT to create customized training materials for your sales team, ensuring they have the skills, knowledge, and confidence needed to close deals and drive revenue.

8. Referral programs: Employ ChatGPT to develop and implement customer referral programs that incentivize your existing customers to refer new clients, helping to drive organic growth and increase customer acquisition.

9. Sales analytics: Utilize ChatGPT to analyze your sales data, uncovering trends, patterns, and insights that can inform your sales strategy and help your team focus on the most effective tactics.

10. Continuous improvement: Regularly gather feedback from your sales team, customers, and stakeholders to identify areas for improvement in your sales and customer acquisition efforts. Use this feedback to refine your ChatGPT-generated resources and strategies, ensuring that they continue to support your startup's growth and goals.

By incorporating ChatGPT into their sales and customer acquisition efforts, startups can create more targeted, persuasive, and personalized sales strategies that resonate with their audience and drive conversions. This not only helps startups differentiate themselves from the competition but also contributes to their long-term success and growth.

Chapter 21: Enhancing Product Development and Innovation

In this chapter, we will explore how startups can leverage ChatGPT to improve their product development and innovation efforts. By utilizing ChatGPT's natural language processing and understanding capabilities, startups can generate new ideas, validate product concepts, and optimize their development processes, leading to the creation of more successful and competitive products.

1. Idea generation: Utilize ChatGPT to generate new product ideas and feature suggestions based on industry trends, customer feedback, and competitive analysis. This can help your startup identify untapped opportunities and drive innovation.

2. Concept validation: Leverage ChatGPT to validate product concepts by conducting market research, analyzing customer feedback, and simulating potential use cases. This can help your startup prioritize the most promising ideas and minimize the risk of investing in unsuccessful products.

3. User experience (UX) design: Use ChatGPT to develop user-centered design principles and guidelines, ensuring that your products are intuitive, engaging, and tailored to your target audience's needs and preferences.

4. Product roadmapping: Employ ChatGPT to create detailed product roadmaps that outline your startup's development plans, milestones, and priorities. This can help ensure that your team remains focused and aligned on your product goals and objectives.

5. Collaborative brainstorming: Utilize ChatGPT to facilitate collaborative brainstorming sessions, generating new ideas,

identifying potential challenges, and uncovering innovative solutions to your product development challenges.

6. Prototype testing: Leverage ChatGPT to design and conduct prototype testing, collecting user feedback and identifying areas for improvement to optimize your product's design, functionality, and performance.

7. Quality assurance: Use ChatGPT to develop and implement rigorous quality assurance processes, ensuring that your products meet or exceed customer expectations and adhere to industry standards and regulations.

8. Product documentation: Employ ChatGPT to create comprehensive product documentation, including user guides, technical specifications, and FAQs. This can help ensure that your customers have the necessary resources and support to use your products effectively.

9. Product launch planning: Utilize ChatGPT to develop a strategic product launch plan, outlining your marketing, sales, and customer support strategies, as well as any post-launch product updates and enhancements.

10. Continuous improvement: Regularly gather feedback from customers, employees, and stakeholders to identify areas for improvement in your product development and innovation efforts. Use this feedback to refine your ChatGPT-generated resources and strategies, ensuring that they continue to support your startup's growth and goals.

By incorporating ChatGPT into their product development and innovation efforts, startups can generate new ideas, validate product concepts, and optimize their development processes. This not only helps startups create more successful and competitive products but also contributes to their long-term success and growth.

Chapter 22: Improving Customer Support and Satisfaction

In this chapter, we will explore how startups can leverage ChatGPT to enhance their customer support and satisfaction efforts. By utilizing ChatGPT's natural language processing and understanding capabilities, startups can provide more responsive, personalized, and efficient support, leading to increased customer loyalty, retention, and advocacy.

1. Chatbot development: Utilize ChatGPT to create AI-powered chatbots that can handle routine customer inquiries, resolve issues, and provide personalized recommendations. This can help reduce response times, improve customer satisfaction, and free up your support team to focus on more complex issues.

2. Knowledge base creation: Leverage ChatGPT to develop a comprehensive and user-friendly knowledge base, featuring articles, tutorials, and FAQs that address common customer questions and concerns. This can help empower customers to find the information they need quickly and efficiently, reducing support requests.

3. Support ticket triaging: Use ChatGPT to automatically triage and categorize incoming support tickets, ensuring that they are routed to the appropriate team members and addressed in a timely manner.

4. Personalized support: Employ ChatGPT to analyze customer data and preferences, enabling your support team to provide personalized and tailored assistance that addresses each customer's unique needs and concerns.

5. Proactive support: Utilize ChatGPT to monitor customer

behavior and identify potential issues before they escalate, allowing your support team to proactively reach out and offer assistance.

6. Multi-channel support: Leverage ChatGPT to manage and streamline support across multiple channels, including email, chat, social media, and phone, ensuring that customers can easily access assistance through their preferred communication method.

7. Customer feedback analysis: Use ChatGPT to analyze customer feedback, including support ticket data, survey responses, and social media comments, identifying trends, patterns, and areas for improvement in your support processes and offerings.

8. Employee training: Employ ChatGPT to create customized training materials for your support team, ensuring that they have the skills, knowledge, and tools needed to provide exceptional customer service.

9. Support performance metrics: Utilize ChatGPT to develop and track key performance indicators (KPIs) for your support team, such as response time, resolution rate, and customer satisfaction scores. This can help you identify areas for improvement and ensure that your team is consistently meeting or exceeding customer expectations.

10. Continuous improvement: Regularly gather feedback from customers, support team members, and stakeholders to identify areas for improvement in your customer support and satisfaction efforts. Use this feedback to refine your ChatGPT-generated resources and strategies, ensuring that they continue to support your startup's growth and goals.

By incorporating ChatGPT into their customer support and satisfaction efforts, startups can provide more responsive, personalized, and efficient support, leading to increased customer loyalty, retention, and advocacy. This not only helps startups differentiate themselves from the competition but also contributes to their long-term success and growth.

Chapter 23: Streamlining Human Resources and Talent Management

In this chapter, we will explore how startups can leverage ChatGPT to optimize their human resources (HR) and talent management efforts. By utilizing ChatGPT's natural language processing and understanding capabilities, startups can attract, retain, and develop top talent, fostering a high-performing and engaged workforce that drives business success.

1. Job description creation: Utilize ChatGPT to craft compelling and accurate job descriptions that clearly outline the responsibilities, qualifications, and expectations for each role, helping to attract the right candidates and streamline the recruitment process.

2. Candidate screening and assessment: Leverage ChatGPT to automate candidate screening and assessment, using AI-powered tools to evaluate resumes, cover letters, and other application materials for relevant skills, experience, and cultural fit.

3. Interview preparation: Use ChatGPT to generate interview questions and evaluation criteria tailored to each role and candidate, ensuring a consistent and objective assessment of applicants.

4. Employee onboarding: Employ ChatGPT to create customized onboarding materials, including orientation schedules, training resources, and new hire checklists, helping to ensure a smooth and successful transition for new employees.

5. Performance management: Utilize ChatGPT to develop and implement performance management processes, including

goal setting, performance reviews, and feedback mechanisms, fostering a culture of continuous improvement and growth.

6. Employee engagement: Leverage ChatGPT to design and execute employee engagement initiatives, such as team-building activities, recognition programs, and feedback sessions, helping to increase employee satisfaction, retention, and productivity.

7. Learning and development: Use ChatGPT to create personalized learning and development plans for each employee, identifying skill gaps, professional interests, and growth opportunities, and providing tailored resources and support.

8. Succession planning: Employ ChatGPT to identify and develop high-potential employees for future leadership roles, ensuring a strong pipeline of talent and continuity in your startup's growth and success.

9. HR analytics: Utilize ChatGPT to analyze HR data and metrics, uncovering trends, patterns, and insights that can inform your talent management strategy and help you optimize your workforce's performance and potential.

10. Continuous improvement: Regularly gather feedback from employees, managers, and stakeholders to identify areas for improvement in your HR and talent management efforts. Use this feedback to refine your ChatGPT-generated resources and strategies, ensuring that they continue to support your startup's growth and goals.

By incorporating ChatGPT into their HR and talent management efforts, startups can attract, retain, and develop top talent, fostering a high-performing and engaged workforce that drives business success. This not only helps startups differentiate themselves from the competition but also contributes to their long-term success and growth.

Chapter 24: Enhancing Marketing and Branding Efforts

In this chapter, we will explore how startups can leverage ChatGPT to boost their marketing and branding efforts. By utilizing ChatGPT's natural language processing and understanding capabilities, startups can create more compelling, targeted, and engaging marketing campaigns that resonate with their audience and drive growth.

1. Content creation: Utilize ChatGPT to generate high-quality, SEO-friendly content for your startup's blog, social media, and other marketing channels, helping to increase brand visibility, establish thought leadership, and drive traffic to your website.

2. Social media management: Leverage ChatGPT to craft engaging social media posts, monitor engagement, and respond to comments and messages in a timely and personalized manner, fostering a strong and loyal online community.

3. Email marketing: Use ChatGPT to create targeted and personalized email campaigns, including newsletters, promotional offers, and nurture sequences, driving engagement, conversions, and customer loyalty.

4. Advertising copy: Employ ChatGPT to write persuasive ad copy for your startup's paid advertising campaigns, such as Google Ads, Facebook Ads, and display ads, maximizing your return on investment and driving more qualified leads to your website.

5. Brand storytelling: Utilize ChatGPT to develop a compelling and authentic brand story that resonates with

your target audience, effectively communicating your startup's mission, values, and unique selling propositions.

6. Press releases and public relations: Leverage ChatGPT to craft press releases and other public relations materials that generate media interest and coverage, increasing your startup's visibility and credibility.

7. Marketing strategy development: Use ChatGPT to analyze your startup's marketing performance, customer data, and industry trends, informing the development of a comprehensive and data-driven marketing strategy that aligns with your business goals and objectives.

8. Influencer and affiliate marketing: Employ ChatGPT to identify potential influencer and affiliate partners, craft tailored outreach messages, and develop mutually beneficial partnerships that help to expand your startup's reach and audience.

9. Event marketing: Utilize ChatGPT to plan, promote, and execute both online and offline marketing events, such as webinars, trade shows, and product launches, driving brand awareness and customer engagement.

10. Continuous improvement: Regularly gather feedback from customers, employees, and stakeholders to identify areas for improvement in your marketing and branding efforts. Use this feedback to refine your ChatGPT-generated resources and strategies, ensuring that they continue to support your startup's growth and goals.

By incorporating ChatGPT into their marketing and branding efforts, startups can create more compelling, targeted, and engaging marketing campaigns that resonate with their audience and drive growth. This not only helps startups differentiate themselves from the competition but also contributes to their long-term success and growth.

Chapter 26: Monetizing ChatGPT-Powered Proofreading Services for Startups

In this chapter, we will explore how startups can generate revenue by offering ChatGPT-powered proofreading services. By leveraging ChatGPT's natural language processing and understanding capabilities, startups can provide fast, accurate, and cost-effective proofreading services to clients, helping them improve the quality of their written content and communications.

1. Develop a proofreading service platform: Create a user-friendly platform that allows clients to easily submit their documents for proofreading. Integrate ChatGPT into the platform to handle the majority of the proofreading tasks, while maintaining a team of human proofreaders to handle more complex or nuanced edits.

2. Target specific industries and niches: Identify industries and niches that have a high demand for proofreading services, such as academia, publishing, legal, and marketing. Tailor your ChatGPT-powered proofreading services to cater to the specific needs and requirements of these industries.

3. Offer multiple pricing tiers: Provide different pricing tiers based on the turnaround time, document length, and level of editing required. This will cater to a wider range of clients and increase the chances of converting potential customers.

4. Bundle with other services: Create service bundles that combine proofreading with other related services, such as content creation, translation, or transcription. This can help your startup stand out from the competition and increase the value proposition for clients.

5. Promote your proofreading services: Implement a strategic

marketing plan to promote your ChatGPT-powered proofreading services, targeting your identified industries and niches through targeted advertising, social media campaigns, and content marketing.

6. Establish a strong online presence: Create a professional and user-friendly website that showcases your startup's proofreading services, highlighting the benefits of using ChatGPT-powered proofreading, such as faster turnaround times, improved accuracy, and cost savings.

7. Provide exceptional customer service: Ensure that your startup provides top-notch customer service, including prompt and efficient communication, clear explanations of the proofreading process, and a streamlined feedback system for clients to express any concerns or request revisions.

8. Build a reputation for quality: Consistently deliver high-quality proofreading services, ensuring that your ChatGPT-powered proofreading platform meets or exceeds industry standards and client expectations. This will help build trust and credibility, leading to increased client retention and referrals.

9. Monitor industry trends and advancements: Stay up-to-date with the latest advancements in ChatGPT and natural language processing technology, incorporating any relevant improvements into your proofreading platform to ensure that your startup remains competitive and at the forefront of the industry.

10. Analyze and optimize your proofreading services: Regularly gather feedback from clients, employees, and stakeholders to identify areas for improvement in your ChatGPT-powered proofreading services. Use this feedback to refine your platform, pricing, and marketing strategies, ensuring that they continue to support your startup's growth and revenue

generation goals.

By offering ChatGPT-powered proofreading services, startups can tap into a lucrative market and generate revenue while helping clients improve the quality of their written content and communications. This not only helps startups differentiate themselves from the competition but also contributes to their long-term success and growth.

Chapter 27: Monetizing Real Estate Services with ChatGPT for Startups

In this chapter, we will explore how startups can generate revenue by offering real estate services powered by ChatGPT. By leveraging ChatGPT's natural language processing and understanding capabilities, startups can provide innovative and efficient real estate solutions that cater to the needs of buyers, sellers, renters, and property managers.

1. Develop a real estate chatbot: Create a user-friendly chatbot powered by ChatGPT that can handle inquiries related to property listings, market trends, and neighborhood information. The chatbot can help users find relevant listings, schedule property viewings, and answer common questions, streamlining the property search process and reducing the workload for real estate agents.

2. Personalized property recommendations: Use ChatGPT to analyze user preferences, needs, and search history, generating personalized property recommendations that align with their requirements. This can help increase client satisfaction and conversion rates, leading to higher revenue for your startup.

3. Real estate content creation: Leverage ChatGPT to create high-quality, engaging, and SEO-friendly content for your real estate website and blog. This can help drive traffic to your website, improve search engine rankings, and establish your startup as a trusted source of real estate information.

4. Automated listing descriptions: Utilize ChatGPT to generate compelling and accurate property listing descriptions, saving time for real estate agents and ensuring consistent, high-quality content across all listings.

5. Market analysis and reports: Employ ChatGPT to analyze real estate market data and generate user-friendly reports that provide insights into market trends, pricing, and neighborhood demographics. These reports can be offered as a value-added service to clients or used to inform your startup's marketing and sales strategies.

6. Virtual property tours: Integrate ChatGPT with virtual reality (VR) or 3D imaging technology to create immersive and interactive virtual property tours. This can help attract more potential buyers or renters, reduce the need for in-person viewings, and set your startup apart from competitors.

7. Offer premium services: Provide premium real estate services, such as personalized property search assistance, negotiation support, and transaction management, powered by ChatGPT. Charge clients a premium fee for these services, generating additional revenue for your startup.

8. Partner with other real estate professionals: Establish partnerships with other real estate professionals, such as mortgage brokers, home inspectors, and property managers, to offer a comprehensive suite of real estate services to clients. Your ChatGPT-powered platform can facilitate seamless communication and coordination between all parties involved.

9. Target specific niches: Focus on specific niches within the real estate market, such as luxury properties, investment properties, or vacation rentals, and tailor your ChatGPT-powered services to cater to the unique needs of these niches.

10. Continuous improvement: Regularly gather feedback from clients, employees, and stakeholders to identify areas for improvement in your ChatGPT-powered real estate services. Use this feedback to refine your platform, pricing, and marketing strategies, ensuring that they continue to support

your startup's growth and revenue generation goals.

By offering innovative and efficient real estate services powered by ChatGPT, startups can tap into a lucrative market and generate revenue while helping clients navigate the complex world of real estate transactions. This not only helps startups differentiate themselves from the competition but also contributes to their long-term success and growth.

Chapter 28: Monetizing Gaming and Entertainment with ChatGPT for Startups

In this chapter, we will explore how startups can generate revenue by incorporating ChatGPT into gaming and entertainment solutions. By leveraging ChatGPT's natural language processing and understanding capabilities, startups can create engaging, interactive, and immersive experiences for users, driving growth and revenue in the gaming and entertainment sectors.

1. Develop narrative-driven games: Create games with rich, dynamic storylines and character development powered by ChatGPT. This can help generate a more immersive gaming experience for players, leading to increased engagement, in-game purchases, and positive word-of-mouth marketing.

2. In-game NPC interactions: Utilize ChatGPT to develop intelligent and responsive non-player characters (NPCs) that can engage in realistic conversations with players, providing a more immersive and interactive gaming experience that sets your startup apart from competitors.

3. Customizable in-game content: Leverage ChatGPT to generate personalized in-game content, such as quests, dialogues, and backstory, based on player preferences and in-game choices. This can help increase player engagement and retention, driving revenue through in-game purchases and subscriptions.

4. ChatGPT-powered game guides and walkthroughs: Create comprehensive and up-to-date game guides and walkthroughs using ChatGPT, providing players with valuable resources that can help them navigate and succeed in your games. Offer these resources as a premium service or as

part of a subscription package.

5. Interactive storytelling platforms: Develop a platform that allows users to create and share interactive, branching stories powered by ChatGPT. Charge users a subscription fee to access premium features, such as advanced editing tools, additional story templates, and increased storage space.

6. Virtual event hosting: Integrate ChatGPT into virtual event platforms, allowing users to host immersive and interactive virtual events, such as concerts, conferences, and festivals. Charge users a fee for hosting events, selling virtual tickets, or accessing premium event features.

7. ChatGPT-powered virtual assistants for gaming and entertainment: Create virtual assistants powered by ChatGPT that can help users discover new games, movies, and entertainment content based on their preferences and interests. Offer these virtual assistants as part of a subscription service or as a value-added feature for premium users.

8. Content creation for entertainment platforms: Utilize ChatGPT to generate high-quality, engaging, and SEO-friendly content for entertainment platforms, such as blogs, podcasts, and video channels. This can help drive traffic to your platform, improve search engine rankings, and generate advertising revenue.

9. Ad integration and in-game purchases: Incorporate in-game advertising and in-game purchase opportunities into your ChatGPT-powered gaming and entertainment solutions. This can help generate additional revenue streams for your startup while providing users with an engaging and interactive experience.

10. Continuous improvement: Regularly gather feedback from users, employees, and stakeholders to identify areas for

improvement in your ChatGPT-powered gaming and entertainment solutions. Use this feedback to refine your platform, pricing, and marketing strategies, ensuring that they continue to support your startup's growth and revenue generation goals.

By incorporating ChatGPT into gaming and entertainment solutions, startups can create engaging, interactive, and immersive experiences for users, driving growth and revenue in these sectors. This not only helps startups differentiate themselves from the competition but also contributes to their long-term success and growth.

Chapter 29: Monetizing AI-Driven Finance Services with ChatGPT for Startups

In this chapter, we will explore how startups can generate revenue by offering AI-driven finance services powered by ChatGPT. By leveraging ChatGPT's natural language processing and understanding capabilities, startups can provide innovative, efficient, and personalized financial solutions that cater to the needs of individuals and businesses alike.

1. Develop a financial chatbot: Create a user-friendly chatbot powered by ChatGPT that can handle inquiries related to personal finance, investments, loans, and more. The chatbot can help users find relevant financial products, answer common questions, and provide personalized financial advice, streamlining the decision-making process for clients and reducing the workload for financial advisors.

2. Personalized investment recommendations: Use ChatGPT to analyze user preferences, risk tolerance, and financial goals, generating personalized investment recommendations that align with their requirements. This can help increase client satisfaction and conversion rates, leading to higher revenue for your startup.

3. Automated financial planning: Leverage ChatGPT to develop an automated financial planning platform that helps users create customized financial plans, set savings goals, and track their progress. Offer this platform as a subscription service or as part of a premium financial advisory package.

4. AI-driven credit scoring and risk assessment: Utilize ChatGPT to create a more accurate and efficient credit scoring and risk assessment system for lending institutions.

This can help improve loan approval rates, reduce default risk, and streamline the loan application process for clients.

5. Fraud detection and prevention: Employ ChatGPT to analyze transaction data and detect patterns indicative of fraudulent activity. Offer this fraud detection and prevention service to financial institutions, helping them reduce losses and maintain customer trust.

6. Financial content creation: Use ChatGPT to generate high-quality, engaging, and SEO-friendly financial content for your startup's website, blog, or social media channels. This can help drive traffic to your platform, improve search engine rankings, and establish your startup as a trusted source of financial information.

7. AI-powered financial analysis and reporting: Leverage ChatGPT to analyze financial data and generate user-friendly reports that provide insights into market trends, investment performance, and financial health. Offer these reports as a value-added service to clients or use them to inform your startup's financial advisory services.

8. Tax and accounting services: Integrate ChatGPT into tax preparation and accounting software, enabling users to receive personalized tax advice, streamline the tax filing process, and optimize their financial strategies. Offer these services as part of a subscription package or as a standalone product.

9. Financial education and coaching: Develop ChatGPT-powered financial education and coaching programs, helping users improve their financial literacy and make more informed financial decisions. Charge clients a fee for access to these programs or offer them as part of a premium financial advisory package.

10. Continuous improvement: Regularly gather feedback from

clients, employees, and stakeholders to identify areas for improvement in your ChatGPT-powered finance services. Use this feedback to refine your platform, pricing, and marketing strategies, ensuring that they continue to support your startup's growth and revenue generation goals.

By offering AI-driven finance services powered by ChatGPT, startups can tap into a lucrative market and generate revenue while helping clients make informed financial decisions and achieve their financial goals. This not only helps startups differentiate themselves from the competition but also contributes to their long-term success and growth.

Chapter 30: Monetizing Travel and Tourism Services with ChatGPT for Startups

In this chapter, we will explore how startups can generate revenue by offering travel and tourism services powered by ChatGPT. By leveraging ChatGPT's natural language processing and understanding capabilities, startups can provide innovative, efficient, and personalized travel solutions that cater to the needs of tourists and travelers alike.

1. Develop a travel chatbot: Create a user-friendly chatbot powered by ChatGPT that can handle inquiries related to flights, accommodations, tours, and more. The chatbot can help users find relevant travel options, answer common questions, and provide personalized travel recommendations, streamlining the decision-making process for clients and reducing the workload for travel agents.

2. Personalized trip planning: Use ChatGPT to analyze user preferences, interests, and travel history, generating personalized trip itineraries that align with their requirements. Offer this trip planning service as a standalone product or as part of a premium travel advisory package.

3. Automated travel content creation: Leverage ChatGPT to generate high-quality, engaging, and SEO-friendly travel content for your startup's website, blog, or social media channels. This can help drive traffic to your platform, improve search engine rankings, and generate advertising revenue.

4. AI-driven travel recommendations: Utilize ChatGPT to create a travel recommendation engine that suggests destinations, attractions, and activities based on user

preferences and interests. Offer these recommendations as a value-added service to clients or use them to inform your startup's travel advisory services.

5. Virtual travel experiences: Integrate ChatGPT with virtual reality (VR) or augmented reality (AR) technology to create immersive and interactive virtual travel experiences. Offer these experiences as a standalone product or as part of a subscription package, allowing users to explore destinations before they commit to booking a trip.

6. Language translation and cultural assistance: Employ ChatGPT to provide real-time language translation and cultural assistance for travelers, helping them navigate language barriers and better understand local customs and traditions. Offer this service as a standalone product or as part of a premium travel advisory package.

7. Travel booking platform: Develop a ChatGPT-powered travel booking platform that allows users to search for and book flights, accommodations, tours, and activities. Integrate chatbot functionality to streamline the booking process and offer personalized recommendations based on user preferences.

8. Partner with travel providers: Establish partnerships with airlines, hotels, tour operators, and other travel providers to offer exclusive deals and discounts to clients who book through your ChatGPT-powered platform. This can help generate additional revenue streams for your startup and provide users with a more comprehensive and cost-effective travel experience.

9. Customer support and assistance: Utilize ChatGPT to offer customer support and assistance for travelers, helping them address issues and concerns that may arise during their trips. Charge clients a fee for access to this support service or offer

it as part of a premium travel advisory package.

10. Continuous improvement: Regularly gather feedback from clients, employees, and stakeholders to identify areas for improvement in your ChatGPT-powered travel and tourism services. Use this feedback to refine your platform, pricing, and marketing strategies, ensuring that they continue to support your startup's growth and revenue generation goals.

By offering innovative and personalized travel and tourism services powered by ChatGPT, startups can tap into a lucrative market and generate revenue while helping clients create unforgettable travel experiences. This not only helps startups differentiate themselves from the competition but also contributes to their long-term success and growth.

Chapter 31: Monetizing AI-Driven Event Planning with ChatGPT for Startups and the Benefits

In this chapter, we will explore how startups can generate revenue by offering AI-driven event planning services powered by ChatGPT. We will also discuss the benefits of using ChatGPT for event planning and how it can contribute to the success of a startup in the event management industry.

1. Develop an event planning chatbot: Create a user-friendly chatbot powered by ChatGPT that can handle inquiries related to venue selection, catering options, entertainment, and more. The chatbot can help users find relevant event planning options, answer common questions, and provide personalized recommendations, streamlining the decision-making process for clients and reducing the workload for event planners.

2. Personalized event itineraries: Use ChatGPT to analyze user preferences, event objectives, and guest profiles, generating personalized event itineraries that align with the client's requirements. Offer this service as a standalone product or as part of a premium event planning package.

3. AI-driven vendor recommendations: Leverage ChatGPT to create a vendor recommendation engine that suggests suitable vendors for various event services, such as catering, entertainment, and decorations, based on user preferences, budget, and location. Offer these recommendations as a value-added service to clients or use them to inform your startup's event planning services.

4. Automated event content creation: Utilize ChatGPT to

generate high-quality, engaging, and SEO-friendly event-related content for your startup's website, blog, or social media channels. This can help drive traffic to your platform, improve search engine rankings, and generate advertising revenue.

5. Virtual event experiences: Integrate ChatGPT with virtual reality (VR) or augmented reality (AR) technology to create immersive and interactive virtual event experiences. Offer these experiences as a standalone product or as part of a subscription package, allowing users to explore venues and event setups before committing to booking.

6. AI-driven event promotion: Employ ChatGPT to create targeted marketing and advertising campaigns that promote events to relevant audiences. Utilize data-driven insights to optimize your campaigns, ensuring maximum reach and engagement.

7. Partner with event service providers: Establish partnerships with venues, caterers, entertainers, and other event service providers to offer exclusive deals and discounts to clients who book through your ChatGPT-powered platform. This can help generate additional revenue streams for your startup and provide users with a more comprehensive and cost-effective event planning experience.

8. Customer support and assistance: Use ChatGPT to offer customer support and assistance for event organizers, helping them address issues and concerns that may arise during the event planning process. Charge clients a fee for access to this support service or offer it as part of a premium event planning package.

Benefits of AI-Driven Event Planning with ChatGPT:

A. Enhanced personalization: ChatGPT's ability to understand user preferences and requirements allows for highly personalized event planning services, resulting in improved client satisfaction and increased loyalty.

B. Improved efficiency: By automating various aspects of event planning, such as vendor recommendations and content creation, startups can reduce the workload for their team and allocate resources more effectively.

C. Cost savings: AI-driven event planning solutions can help startups reduce operational costs by automating tasks that would otherwise require manual intervention.

D. Competitive advantage: By offering innovative and personalized event planning services powered by ChatGPT, startups can differentiate themselves from competitors and position themselves as industry leaders.

E. Data-driven insights: ChatGPT-powered event planning solutions can provide startups with valuable data and insights, enabling them to make informed decisions, optimize their services, and drive business growth.

By offering AI-driven event planning services powered by ChatGPT, startups can tap into a lucrative market and generate revenue while providing clients with exceptional

Chapter 32: Monetizing ChatGPT-Powered Personal Assistants for Startups and the Benefits

In this chapter, we will explore how startups can generate revenue by offering ChatGPT-powered personal assistant services. We will also discuss the benefits of using ChatGPT for personal assistant services and how it can contribute to the success of a startup in the AI-driven personal assistant industry.

1. Develop a personal assistant chatbot: Create a user-friendly chatbot powered by ChatGPT that can handle a wide range of tasks, including scheduling appointments, making reservations, managing to-do lists, and providing reminders. The chatbot can help users stay organized and efficient, reducing the workload for human personal assistants and saving clients time and effort.

2. Offer premium personal assistant packages: Use ChatGPT to develop a tiered personal assistant subscription service, with premium packages offering additional features and capabilities, such as in-depth research, personalized recommendations, and priority support. This can help attract a diverse range of clients and generate recurring revenue for your startup.

3. AI-driven lifestyle recommendations: Leverage ChatGPT to create a recommendation engine that suggests personalized lifestyle options, such as fitness routines, meal plans, and leisure activities, based on user preferences and goals. Offer these recommendations as a value-added service to clients or use them to inform your startup's personal assistant services.

4. Virtual coaching and mentoring: Integrate ChatGPT with

virtual coaching and mentoring programs, helping users improve their skills, achieve their goals, and enhance their overall well-being. Offer these programs as a standalone product or as part of a premium personal assistant package.

5. Language translation and cultural assistance: Utilize ChatGPT to provide real-time language translation and cultural assistance for users who travel or work in multicultural environments. Offer this service as a standalone product or as part of a premium personal assistant package.

6. Partner with service providers: Establish partnerships with various service providers, such as restaurants, fitness centers, and transportation services, to offer exclusive deals and discounts to clients who book through your ChatGPT-powered personal assistant platform. This can help generate additional revenue streams for your startup and provide users with a more comprehensive and cost-effective personal assistant experience.

Benefits of ChatGPT-Powered Personal Assistants:

A. Enhanced personalization: ChatGPT's ability to understand user preferences and requirements allows for highly personalized personal assistant services, resulting in improved client satisfaction and increased loyalty.

B. Improved efficiency: By automating various aspects of personal assistance, such as scheduling and reminders, startups can reduce the workload for their team and allocate resources more effectively.

C. Cost savings: AI-driven personal assistant solutions can help startups reduce operational costs by automating tasks that would otherwise require manual intervention.

D. Competitive advantage: By offering innovative and personalized personal assistant services powered by ChatGPT, startups can differentiate themselves from competitors and position themselves as industry leaders.

E. Data-driven insights: ChatGPT-powered personal assistant solutions can provide startups with valuable data and insights, enabling them to make informed decisions, optimize their services, and drive business growth.

By offering ChatGPT-powered personal assistant services, startups can tap into a lucrative market and generate revenue while providing clients with exceptional and personalized assistance. This not only helps startups differentiate themselves from the competition but also contributes to their long-term success and growth.

Chapter 33: Monetizing News and Media Content Generation with ChatGPT for Startups

In this chapter, we will explore how startups can generate revenue by offering news and media content generation services powered by ChatGPT. Leveraging the capabilities of ChatGPT in natural language processing and understanding, startups can provide innovative, efficient, and high-quality news and media content that caters to the diverse needs of their target audience.

1. Develop a news and media content chatbot: Create a user-friendly chatbot powered by ChatGPT that can handle inquiries related to the latest news, trending topics, and media content. The chatbot can help users find relevant articles, videos, and podcasts, as well as answer questions and provide summaries of important events, streamlining the content consumption experience for users.

2. Automated news and media content creation: Utilize ChatGPT to generate high-quality, engaging, and SEO-friendly news articles, blog posts, and other media content for your startup's website, app, or social media channels. This can help drive traffic to your platform, improve search engine rankings, and generate advertising revenue.

3. Personalized news and media recommendations: Leverage ChatGPT to create a recommendation engine that suggests news and media content based on user preferences, interests, and reading history. Offer these recommendations as a value-added service to users or use them to inform your startup's content curation strategy.

4. AI-driven content curation: Employ ChatGPT to analyze

and filter large volumes of news and media content, identifying the most relevant and high-quality pieces for your target audience. Use this curated content to populate your platform, app, or social media channels, attracting users and generating advertising revenue.

5. Fact-checking and content verification: Integrate ChatGPT with fact-checking algorithms and resources to create an AI-powered fact-checking service for news and media content. Offer this service to clients, such as journalists, bloggers, and media organizations, to ensure the accuracy and credibility of their content.

6. AI-driven news and media analytics: Utilize ChatGPT to analyze user engagement, content performance, and other relevant metrics, providing insights that can help inform your startup's content strategy, marketing campaigns, and overall business direction.

7. Subscription-based news and media platform: Develop a ChatGPT-powered news and media platform that offers users access to exclusive content, personalized recommendations, and additional features through a subscription model. This can help generate recurring revenue for your startup and foster user loyalty.

8. Partner with news and media organizations: Establish partnerships with news agencies, media organizations, and content creators to offer exclusive content, collaborative projects, or advertising opportunities through your ChatGPT-powered platform. This can help generate additional revenue streams for your startup and provide users with a more comprehensive and diverse content experience.

9. Custom content solutions for businesses: Offer ChatGPT-powered content creation services to businesses and organizations that require news articles, blog posts, or other

media content for their websites, apps, or marketing campaigns. Charge clients on a per-piece or project basis, generating revenue for your startup.

By offering innovative and personalized news and media content generation services powered by ChatGPT, startups can tap into a lucrative market and generate revenue while providing users with high-quality, relevant, and engaging content. This not only helps startups differentiate themselves from the competition but also contributes to their long-term success and growth.

Chapter 34: Monetizing Smart City Solutions for Startups

In this chapter, we will explore how startups can generate revenue by offering smart city solutions. As urban populations grow and cities face challenges related to infrastructure, energy, transportation, and environmental sustainability, startups can leverage innovative technologies to develop solutions that improve urban living and create more efficient, sustainable, and resilient cities.

1. Intelligent transportation systems: Develop smart transportation solutions that use real-time data, sensors, and AI algorithms to optimize traffic flow, reduce congestion, and improve public transit efficiency. Offer these solutions to city governments, transportation agencies, and private sector clients to generate revenue.

2. Smart energy management: Create energy management solutions that leverage IoT devices, sensors, and AI to monitor and optimize energy consumption in buildings, public spaces, and infrastructure. Offer these solutions to property owners, facility managers, and city governments to help them reduce energy costs and meet sustainability goals.

3. Waste management and recycling: Develop smart waste management and recycling solutions that use sensors, data analytics, and AI to optimize collection routes, monitor waste levels, and promote recycling efforts. Offer these services to city governments and waste management companies to generate revenue.

4. Environmental monitoring and pollution control: Create solutions that use IoT devices, sensors, and AI to monitor air and water quality, detect pollution sources, and provide real-

time data to city governments and environmental agencies. Offer these solutions as a service to help cities improve public health and meet environmental regulations.

5. Smart public safety and security: Develop public safety and security solutions that leverage AI, data analytics, and IoT devices to monitor city spaces, detect potential threats, and coordinate emergency response efforts. Offer these solutions to city governments and law enforcement agencies to generate revenue.

6. E-governance and citizen engagement: Create e-governance platforms that use AI, data analytics, and digital technologies to streamline government services, improve transparency, and facilitate citizen participation in decision-making processes. Offer these platforms to city governments as a subscription service or on a project basis.

7. Smart urban planning and development: Develop smart urban planning and development tools that use AI, data analytics, and digital technologies to analyze urban data, simulate development scenarios, and optimize land use, zoning, and infrastructure planning. Offer these tools to city governments, urban planners, and real estate developers to generate revenue.

8. IoT-based infrastructure monitoring and maintenance: Create IoT-based solutions that monitor the health and performance of urban infrastructure, such as bridges, roads, and water systems, and use AI to predict maintenance needs and optimize resource allocation. Offer these solutions to city governments and infrastructure management companies to generate revenue.

9. Partner with city governments and private sector clients: Establish partnerships with city governments, private sector clients, and other stakeholders to collaborate on smart city

projects, secure funding, and access valuable data and resources. Offer your smart city solutions as part of a comprehensive package or on a project basis, generating revenue for your startup.

By offering innovative smart city solutions, startups can tap into a growing market and generate revenue while addressing pressing urban challenges and contributing to the development of more sustainable, efficient, and resilient cities. This not only helps startups differentiate themselves from the competition but also contributes to their long-term success and growth.

Chapter 34: Leveraging ChatGPT for Smart City Solutions

In this chapter, we will explore how startups can leverage ChatGPT in their smart city solutions to provide more efficient, user-friendly, and intelligent services.

1. Intelligent transportation systems: Utilize ChatGPT to create conversational interfaces for transportation applications, allowing users to access real-time traffic updates, public transit schedules, and route suggestions using natural language queries.
2. Smart energy management: Develop a ChatGPT-powered chatbot that can assist users in monitoring their energy consumption, providing personalized tips for energy-saving strategies, and answering questions about energy efficiency measures.
3. Waste management and recycling: Integrate ChatGPT into waste management and recycling applications to offer users a conversational interface to receive guidance on proper waste disposal, recycling procedures, and local waste collection schedules.
4. Environmental monitoring and pollution control: Leverage ChatGPT to provide users with natural language access to real-time air and water quality data, as well as information on local environmental initiatives and policies.
5. Smart public safety and security: Use ChatGPT to develop chatbots that can provide users with safety and security information, such as emergency contact numbers, nearby safe zones, and crime prevention tips, in a conversational manner.
6. E-governance and citizen engagement: Implement

ChatGPT-powered chatbots and virtual assistants to facilitate user interaction with government services, allowing citizens to easily access information, submit requests, and provide feedback on local issues.

7. Smart urban planning and development: Integrate ChatGPT into urban planning tools to provide natural language explanations of complex data, simulations, and recommendations, making it easier for urban planners, city officials, and other stakeholders to understand and utilize the information.

8. IoT-based infrastructure monitoring and maintenance: Leverage ChatGPT to create chatbots and virtual assistants that can help infrastructure managers monitor the status of various assets, interpret IoT data, and receive maintenance recommendations in a conversational manner.

9. Partner with city governments and private sector clients: Utilize ChatGPT to develop customized chatbots and virtual assistants for city governments and private sector clients, allowing them to offer their users natural language access to smart city services and information.

By integrating ChatGPT into smart city solutions, startups can provide users with a more intuitive and conversational interface to access services and information. This can not only improve user satisfaction and engagement but also contribute to the overall success and growth of the startup in the smart city market.

Chapter 35: AI-Driven Energy Management Solutions Leveraging ChatGPT

In this chapter, we will explore how startups can develop AI-driven energy management solutions that leverage ChatGPT to provide more efficient, user-friendly, and intelligent services. By combining the power of artificial intelligence with the conversational capabilities of ChatGPT, startups can create innovative energy management solutions that cater to the needs of various stakeholders, including homeowners, facility managers, and city governments.

1. Energy consumption monitoring and analysis: Develop a ChatGPT-powered chatbot that can assist users in monitoring their energy consumption in real-time. This chatbot can analyze energy usage data, identify patterns and trends, and provide insights into the most energy-consuming devices and processes. Users can ask questions and receive tailored recommendations for optimizing energy consumption based on their specific usage patterns.

2. Personalized energy-saving tips: Utilize ChatGPT to create an intelligent assistant that provides personalized energy-saving tips and strategies based on user preferences, habits, and the specific characteristics of their home or building. By offering tailored advice, users can make more informed decisions about their energy consumption and implement targeted energy efficiency measures.

3. Demand response and load balancing: Leverage ChatGPT to create a conversational interface for demand response and load balancing programs. Users can receive notifications about peak demand periods, as well as information on how to

adjust their energy consumption to help balance the grid and reduce energy costs. This can help utilities better manage the electrical grid and ensure a more reliable energy supply.

4. Smart home integration: Integrate ChatGPT with smart home devices and systems, such as smart thermostats, lighting, and appliances, to enable users to control and optimize their energy consumption through natural language commands. Users can interact with their smart home devices using simple voice or text commands, making it easier to manage energy usage and implement energy-saving strategies.

5. Renewable energy management: Develop a ChatGPT-powered virtual assistant that can help users optimize their use of renewable energy sources, such as solar panels and wind turbines. The virtual assistant can provide information on optimal system configuration, real-time energy production data, and advice on maximizing the benefits of renewable energy systems.

6. Facility and building energy management: Create a ChatGPT-powered chatbot that can assist facility managers in monitoring and optimizing energy consumption in commercial and industrial buildings. The chatbot can provide real-time energy usage data, analyze trends, and offer recommendations for implementing energy efficiency measures, such as adjusting HVAC settings, upgrading lighting systems, and optimizing building operations.

7. Energy policy and regulation: Utilize ChatGPT to create a conversational interface for accessing information about energy policies, regulations, and incentives. Users can ask questions about local, regional, and national energy policies, as well as receive guidance on available incentives and programs for energy efficiency and renewable energy projects.

8. User engagement and education: Leverage ChatGPT to

develop engaging and educational content about energy management, efficiency, and conservation. By offering users an interactive and conversational way to learn about energy-related topics, startups can increase user engagement, raise awareness, and promote more sustainable energy practices.

By integrating ChatGPT into AI-driven energy management solutions, startups can offer users a more intuitive and engaging way to monitor, optimize, and control their energy consumption. This not only helps users save on energy costs and reduce their environmental impact but also contributes to the overall success and growth of the startup in the energy management market.

Chapter 36: ChatGPT-Powered Matchmaking Services

In this chapter, we will explore how startups can harness the capabilities of ChatGPT to develop innovative matchmaking services that cater to the diverse needs of people seeking companionship, friendship, or romantic relationships. By leveraging the power of ChatGPT, startups can create more intuitive, personalized, and engaging matchmaking experiences for their users.

1. Personality assessment and compatibility analysis: Develop a ChatGPT-powered chatbot that can conduct personality assessments through engaging, natural language conversations with users. Based on the collected information, the chatbot can analyze compatibility between users and suggest potential matches with high compatibility scores.

2. Personalized match recommendations: Utilize ChatGPT to generate personalized match recommendations based on users' preferences, interests, and values. By offering tailored suggestions, startups can improve the quality of matches and increase the likelihood of successful connections.

3. Conversation starters and icebreakers: Leverage ChatGPT to create conversation starters and icebreakers that can help users initiate conversations with their matches. These conversation prompts can be tailored to users' profiles and interests, making it easier for them to engage in meaningful conversations and build rapport.

4. Relationship advice and support: Integrate ChatGPT into your matchmaking platform to provide users with relationship advice and support. The chatbot can answer questions, offer guidance, and provide resources related to

dating, communication, and relationship building, helping users navigate the complexities of modern relationships.

5. Virtual dating assistants: Develop a ChatGPT-powered virtual dating assistant that can help users create and manage their dating profiles, craft engaging messages, and schedule dates. This virtual assistant can help users optimize their online dating experience and increase their chances of making meaningful connections.

6. AI-driven event planning and matchmaking activities: Utilize ChatGPT to plan and organize virtual or in-person matchmaking events, such as speed dating, mixers, or themed gatherings. By analyzing users' preferences and compatibility, the chatbot can create tailored guest lists and facilitate engaging activities that promote interaction and connection among participants.

7. User feedback and continuous improvement: Leverage ChatGPT to gather user feedback on match recommendations, conversation experiences, and overall satisfaction with the service. This feedback can be used to continuously refine the matchmaking algorithm, improving the quality of matches and user experience over time.

8. Enhancing user safety and privacy: Integrate ChatGPT into your matchmaking platform to help users maintain their safety and privacy. The chatbot can offer guidance on best practices for online dating safety, monitor conversations for inappropriate content, and provide users with tools to report or block users who violate the platform's terms of service.

By incorporating ChatGPT into their matchmaking services, startups can offer users a more personalized, engaging, and supportive dating experience. This not only helps users make more meaningful connections but also contributes to the overall success and growth of the startup in the competitive online dating market.

Chapter 37: Startups Leveraging AI-Driven Dating and Relationship Advice with ChatGPT

In this chapter, we will discuss how startups can leverage ChatGPT to develop AI-driven dating and relationship advice services that cater to the diverse needs of individuals seeking guidance and support in their romantic lives. By harnessing the power of ChatGPT, startups can offer personalized, engaging, and timely advice to users, helping them navigate the complexities of modern dating and relationships.

1. Personalized advice based on user preferences and experiences: Utilize ChatGPT to generate personalized dating and relationship advice based on users' preferences, relationship history, and specific concerns. By offering tailored guidance, startups can address users' unique needs and challenges, helping them make more informed decisions in their romantic lives.

2. Conversation analysis and coaching: Leverage ChatGPT to analyze users' conversations with their romantic interests, identifying areas of improvement and providing actionable feedback. The AI-powered chatbot can offer suggestions for enhancing communication skills, resolving conflicts, and building emotional intimacy, helping users foster stronger connections with their partners.

3. Dating profile optimization: Develop a ChatGPT-powered chatbot that can help users create and optimize their dating profiles. By analyzing users' preferences, interests, and personality traits, the chatbot can offer suggestions for improving profile content, selecting profile pictures, and crafting engaging messages that capture users' unique

qualities.

4. Virtual dating assistant: Integrate ChatGPT into a virtual dating assistant service that can help users manage their online dating accounts, schedule dates, and follow up with potential matches. This AI-driven assistant can streamline the dating process, increasing users' chances of finding meaningful connections.

5. AI-driven relationship therapy: Utilize ChatGPT to create a virtual relationship therapist that can guide users through exercises and discussions aimed at improving relationship dynamics, communication, and emotional connection. By offering personalized therapeutic interventions, startups can help users address their relationship challenges and foster healthier, more satisfying partnerships.

6. Real-time dating and relationship advice: Leverage ChatGPT to provide users with real-time dating and relationship advice through a mobile app or web-based platform. Users can ask questions, receive guidance, and access resources related to dating, relationships, and personal growth, all through a convenient and user-friendly interface.

7. Interactive learning and skill-building: Develop ChatGPT-powered interactive learning modules and exercises that help users build essential dating and relationship skills, such as active listening, empathy, and emotional intelligence. By offering engaging and practical learning experiences, startups can help users improve their interpersonal skills and foster more fulfilling romantic connections.

8. User feedback and service improvement: Integrate ChatGPT into your dating and relationship advice platform to gather user feedback and continuously refine the service. By incorporating users' insights and experiences, startups can improve the quality of advice, enhance user satisfaction, and

drive the growth and success of their business.

By leveraging ChatGPT in AI-driven dating and relationship advice services, startups can offer users personalized, engaging, and supportive guidance to help them navigate the challenges of modern dating and relationships. This not only enhances user satisfaction and fosters more meaningful connections but also contributes to the overall success and growth of the startup in the competitive dating and relationship advice market.

Chapter 38: AI-Driven Parenting and Childcare Assistance Leveraging ChatGPT

In this chapter, we will explore how startups can develop AI-driven parenting and childcare assistance services that leverage ChatGPT to provide valuable guidance, support, and resources for parents and caregivers. By integrating ChatGPT into their services, startups can offer more personalized, engaging, and accessible assistance to help users navigate the complexities of parenting and childcare.

1. Parenting advice and support: Utilize ChatGPT to generate personalized parenting advice based on users' specific concerns, child's age, developmental stage, and unique circumstances. By offering tailored guidance, startups can address parents' unique needs and challenges, helping them make more informed decisions and foster healthier, happier family dynamics.

2. Child development tracking and insights: Develop a ChatGPT-powered chatbot that can assist users in tracking their child's developmental milestones and provide insights into their growth and progress. This chatbot can analyze the collected data, identify patterns and trends, and provide tailored recommendations for supporting the child's development based on their specific needs and abilities.

3. Educational resources and activities: Leverage ChatGPT to curate educational resources and activities that cater to children's interests, learning styles, and developmental stages. By offering personalized and engaging learning experiences, startups can support parents in fostering their children's cognitive, social, and emotional development.

4. Virtual childcare assistant: Integrate ChatGPT into a virtual

childcare assistant service that can help parents manage their childcare responsibilities, such as scheduling appointments, coordinating playdates, and tracking milestones. This AI-driven assistant can streamline the parenting process, increasing users' efficiency and reducing stress.

5. Behavior management and discipline strategies: Utilize ChatGPT to create a conversational interface that provides parents with guidance on effective behavior management and discipline strategies. By offering evidence-based recommendations and personalized support, startups can help parents address behavioral challenges and create a more harmonious family environment.

6. Health and wellness support: Leverage ChatGPT to provide users with information and resources related to their child's health and wellness, such as nutrition, sleep, and mental health. Users can ask questions and receive tailored advice to help them make informed decisions about their child's well-being.

7. Parenting community and support network: Develop a ChatGPT-powered platform that connects parents with other users who share similar experiences, concerns, and interests. By fostering a supportive community, startups can help users exchange advice, resources, and encouragement, enhancing their parenting experience and reducing feelings of isolation.

8. Parenting skill-building and education: Integrate ChatGPT into your parenting and childcare assistance platform to provide users with interactive learning modules and exercises that help them build essential parenting skills, such as communication, empathy, and stress management. By offering engaging and practical learning experiences, startups can help users improve their parenting skills and foster more

fulfilling family relationships.

By incorporating ChatGPT into their AI-driven parenting and childcare assistance services, startups can offer users personalized, engaging, and accessible support to help them navigate the challenges of parenting. This not only enhances user satisfaction and fosters healthier, happier families but also contributes to the overall success and growth of the startup in the competitive parenting and childcare market.

Chapter 39: ChatGPT-Powered Career Counseling and Startups

In this chapter, we will discuss how startups can leverage ChatGPT to develop AI-driven career counseling services that cater to the diverse needs of individuals seeking guidance and support in their professional lives. By harnessing the power of ChatGPT, startups can offer personalized, engaging, and timely advice to users, helping them navigate the complexities of the modern job market and achieve their career goals.

1. Personalized career advice and guidance: Utilize ChatGPT to generate personalized career advice based on users' skills, interests, experiences, and goals. By offering tailored guidance, startups can address users' unique needs and challenges, helping them make more informed decisions and pursue fulfilling career paths.

2. Job search assistance and strategy: Leverage ChatGPT to create a virtual career counselor that can help users develop effective job search strategies, craft compelling resumes and cover letters, and prepare for interviews. By offering actionable tips and insights, startups can increase users' chances of securing employment and achieving their career objectives.

3. Skill assessment and development: Develop a ChatGPT-powered chatbot that can assess users' skills and identify areas for improvement. Based on the collected information, the chatbot can suggest relevant training programs, resources, and activities to help users enhance their skillsets and boost their employability.

4. Career exploration and planning: Integrate ChatGPT into

your career counseling platform to assist users in exploring different career paths and determining the most suitable options based on their interests, values, and abilities. The AI-powered chatbot can also help users create realistic and achievable career plans, setting them on a path to success.

5. Networking and professional development: Utilize ChatGPT to provide users with guidance on networking strategies, personal branding, and professional development opportunities. By offering targeted advice and resources, startups can help users build strong professional networks and advance their careers.

6. Real-time career advice and support: Leverage ChatGPT to offer users real-time career advice and support through a mobile app or web-based platform. Users can ask questions, receive guidance, and access resources related to job searching, career development, and personal growth, all through a convenient and user-friendly interface.

7. Interactive learning and skill-building: Integrate ChatGPT into your career counseling platform to provide users with interactive learning modules and exercises that help them build essential job-related skills, such as communication, problem-solving, and leadership. By offering engaging and practical learning experiences, startups can enhance users' employability and career prospects.

8. User feedback and service improvement: Utilize ChatGPT to gather user feedback on the effectiveness of the career counseling services and continuously refine the platform. By incorporating users' insights and experiences, startups can improve the quality of advice, enhance user satisfaction, and drive the growth and success of their business.

By leveraging ChatGPT in AI-driven career counseling services, startups can offer users personalized, engaging, and supportive guidance to help them navigate the challenges of the modern job market and achieve their career goals. This not only enhances user satisfaction and fosters professional growth but also contributes to the overall success and growth of the startup in the competitive career counseling market.

Chapter 40 : AI-Driven Therapy and Mental Health Services Using ChatGPT

As the demand for mental health services continues to grow, the integration of AI-driven technology, such as ChatGPT, into therapy and mental health services offers a promising solution to bridge the gap between the number of individuals seeking support and the availability of professional care. In this piece, we will explore how ChatGPT can be leveraged to provide personalized, accessible, and effective mental health services to those in need.

1. Personalized therapy and support: By utilizing ChatGPT, mental health startups can offer personalized therapeutic interventions based on users' specific concerns, experiences, and preferences. ChatGPT can analyze users' responses and provide tailored guidance, helping individuals better understand their emotions and thought patterns, and develop effective coping strategies.

2. Real-time emotional support: ChatGPT can be integrated into mental health platforms to offer real-time emotional support, allowing users to access help whenever they need it. The AI-powered chatbot can provide immediate empathy, validation, and encouragement, helping users manage their emotions and navigate challenging situations.

3. Mental health education and self-help resources: Leverage ChatGPT to curate a collection of educational content and self-help resources designed to empower users to take charge of their mental health. The AI-driven chatbot can offer personalized suggestions for articles, videos, and exercises based on users' specific needs and interests.

4. Mood tracking and analysis: Develop a ChatGPT-powered

chatbot that assists users in tracking their mood and emotional patterns over time. By analyzing the collected data, the chatbot can identify trends, triggers, and coping strategies, providing users with valuable insights into their mental health and wellbeing.

5. Cognitive-behavioral therapy (CBT) techniques: Integrate ChatGPT into your mental health platform to provide users with AI-driven CBT techniques designed to help them challenge and reframe negative thoughts and beliefs. By offering guided exercises and interactive activities, startups can support users in developing more adaptive thought patterns and behaviors.

6. Group therapy and peer support: Utilize ChatGPT to create a virtual support group where users can connect with others who share similar experiences and concerns. The AI-powered chatbot can facilitate discussions, offer guidance, and foster a sense of community and connection, helping users feel less isolated and more supported in their mental health journey.

7. Mental health screening and assessment: Leverage ChatGPT to develop a chatbot capable of conducting mental health screenings and assessments, helping users identify potential mental health concerns and directing them to appropriate professional care when necessary.

8. Privacy and ethical considerations: While implementing ChatGPT in mental health services, startups must prioritize user privacy and ethical considerations. Ensure that data is securely stored, and users are informed about the limitations of AI-driven therapy, including the importance of seeking professional care for more severe mental health concerns.

By integrating ChatGPT into therapy and mental health services, startups can provide users with personalized, accessible, and timely support, helping them better manage their mental health and well-being. This not only enhances user satisfaction and fosters improved mental health outcomes but also contributes to the overall success and growth of the startup in the competitive mental health market.

Chapter 41: AI-Driven Sports Analysis and Training Leveraging ChatGPT

In this chapter, we will explore the potential of ChatGPT in revolutionizing sports analysis and training, offering personalized guidance, insights, and support to athletes and coaches at all levels. By harnessing the power of ChatGPT, startups can develop innovative AI-driven sports analysis and training platforms that cater to the diverse needs of users, helping them enhance their performance and achieve their goals.

1. Personalized training programs: Utilize ChatGPT to create personalized training programs for athletes based on their specific goals, strengths, weaknesses, and schedules. By offering tailored guidance and recommendations, startups can help users optimize their training and improve their performance in their chosen sport.

2. Performance analysis and feedback: Leverage ChatGPT to analyze users' performance data, such as workout logs, game statistics, and video footage, and provide insights into areas for improvement, strengths, and weaknesses. The AI-powered chatbot can offer targeted feedback and suggestions for users to enhance their skills and performance.

3. Injury prevention and rehabilitation: Develop a ChatGPT-powered chatbot that can help users identify potential injury risks, suggest appropriate injury prevention strategies, and guide them through the rehabilitation process when necessary. By offering evidence-based recommendations and personalized support, startups can help users maintain their physical health and reduce downtime due to injuries.

4. Mental skills training and sports psychology: Integrate

ChatGPT into your sports analysis and training platform to provide users with mental skills training and sports psychology resources, such as relaxation techniques, visualization exercises, and goal-setting strategies. By offering targeted advice and support, startups can help users develop the mental resilience and focus required for peak performance.

5. Nutritional guidance and meal planning: Utilize ChatGPT to provide users with personalized nutritional guidance and meal planning suggestions based on their sport, training goals, and dietary preferences. By offering tailored advice and resources, startups can support users in optimizing their nutrition for enhanced performance and recovery.

6. Virtual coaching and mentoring: Leverage ChatGPT to create a virtual coaching and mentoring platform where users can connect with experienced athletes and coaches, ask questions, and receive guidance on their training, performance, and career development. By fostering a supportive community, startups can help users enhance their skills, knowledge, and confidence.

7. Interactive learning modules and exercises: Integrate ChatGPT into your sports analysis and training platform to provide users with interactive learning modules and exercises that help them build essential sports-related skills, such as technique, strategy, and decision-making. By offering engaging and practical learning experiences, startups can enhance users' performance and understanding of their chosen sport.

8. Real-time performance tracking and feedback: Utilize ChatGPT to develop a real-time performance tracking and feedback system, allowing users to monitor their progress and receive instant guidance and support during their training

sessions. This AI-driven system can enhance users' motivation and help them make more informed decisions about their training and performance.

By leveraging ChatGPT in AI-driven sports analysis and training services, startups can offer users personalized, engaging, and effective guidance and support to help them enhance their performance and achieve their goals. This not only improves user satisfaction and fosters athletic success but also contributes to the overall growth and success of the startup in the competitive sports analysis and training market.

Chapter 42: ChatGPT-Powered Recipe and Meal Planning Solutions

In this chapter, we will explore the potential of ChatGPT in revolutionizing the culinary landscape by offering AI-driven recipe and meal planning solutions. By harnessing the power of ChatGPT, startups can develop innovative platforms that cater to the diverse needs of users, helping them create delicious and healthy meals while saving time and reducing food waste.

1. Personalized meal planning: Utilize ChatGPT to generate personalized meal plans for users based on their dietary preferences, restrictions, allergies, and health goals. By offering tailored meal plans, startups can help users maintain a balanced and enjoyable diet while addressing their unique nutritional needs.

2. AI-generated recipes: Leverage ChatGPT to create original, customized recipes based on users' ingredient preferences, dietary restrictions, and desired meal types. By offering a wide range of unique and flavorful recipes, startups can inspire users to explore new culinary experiences and expand their cooking repertoire.

3. Ingredient substitution suggestions: Develop a ChatGPT-powered chatbot that can offer ingredient substitution suggestions to users, helping them adapt recipes to accommodate their dietary needs, preferences, or pantry limitations. By offering practical and creative alternatives, startups can help users avoid food waste and make the most of their available ingredients.

4. Cooking techniques and tips: Integrate ChatGPT into your recipe and meal planning platform to provide users with

helpful cooking techniques, tips, and tricks. The AI-driven chatbot can offer guidance on various cooking methods, food preparation techniques, and equipment usage, helping users enhance their culinary skills and confidence.

5. Nutritional analysis and guidance: Utilize ChatGPT to provide users with detailed nutritional information for their chosen recipes and meal plans, helping them make informed decisions about their diet and overall health. The AI-powered chatbot can also offer suggestions for optimizing the nutritional content of users' meals, promoting a balanced and healthy diet.

6. Grocery list generation and optimization: Leverage ChatGPT to generate and optimize grocery lists based on users' selected recipes and meal plans. The AI-driven chatbot can help users identify the most efficient shopping route, suggest pantry staples, and offer tips on selecting the freshest and highest-quality ingredients, ultimately saving users time and money.

7. Community support and recipe sharing: Utilize ChatGPT to create a virtual community where users can share their favorite recipes, cooking tips, and meal planning strategies. The AI-powered chatbot can facilitate discussions, answer questions, and foster a sense of connection among users, encouraging them to learn from one another and expand their culinary horizons.

8. Voice-activated cooking assistance: Integrate ChatGPT into a voice-activated assistant to provide hands-free cooking guidance for users, offering step-by-step instructions, ingredient lists, and cooking tips. This feature can improve users' cooking experience, allowing them to focus on their culinary creations without the need to reference written instructions or juggle multiple devices.

By leveraging ChatGPT in AI-driven recipe and meal planning solutions, startups can offer users personalized, engaging, and practical guidance, helping them create delicious and healthy meals while saving time and reducing food waste. This not only enhances user satisfaction but also contributes to the overall success and growth of the startup in the competitive recipe and meal planning market.

Chapter 43: Startups and AI-Driven Fashion and Style Advice Leveraging ChatGPT

In this chapter, we will explore how startups can harness the power of ChatGPT to revolutionize the fashion industry by offering AI-driven fashion and style advice. By integrating ChatGPT into their platforms, startups can provide personalized, accessible, and on-trend fashion guidance that caters to users' unique preferences, helping them cultivate their personal style and make confident wardrobe choices.

1. Personalized fashion recommendations: Utilize ChatGPT to generate personalized fashion recommendations for users based on their style preferences, body shape, and lifestyle. By offering tailored suggestions, startups can help users discover new brands, trends, and wardrobe essentials that align with their individual tastes and needs.

2. Virtual styling and outfit planning: Leverage ChatGPT to create a virtual styling and outfit planning platform that allows users to upload images of their existing wardrobe, receive styling tips, and generate new outfit combinations. The AI-powered chatbot can offer guidance on how to mix and match clothing items, accessorize, and create versatile looks for various occasions.

3. Trend analysis and forecasting: Integrate ChatGPT into your fashion platform to analyze and forecast fashion trends based on data from social media, runways, and industry reports. By offering users insights into upcoming trends and styles, startups can help them stay ahead of the curve and make informed purchasing decisions.

4. AI-generated fashion content: Utilize ChatGPT to create

engaging and informative fashion content, such as blog posts, articles, and style guides, tailored to users' specific interests and preferences. By offering targeted advice and inspiration, startups can foster a loyal and engaged user base.

5. Virtual fitting and size recommendations: Leverage ChatGPT to develop a virtual fitting and size recommendation system that helps users find the perfect fit when shopping for clothing online. The AI-driven chatbot can offer guidance on sizing, taking into account users' body measurements, brand-specific sizing charts, and user reviews.

6. Sustainable fashion and eco-conscious shopping: Integrate ChatGPT into your fashion platform to provide users with guidance on sustainable fashion choices, including eco-friendly brands, clothing care tips, and strategies for reducing textile waste. By promoting sustainable practices, startups can contribute to a more environmentally responsible fashion industry.

7. Personal shopping and curated collections: Utilize ChatGPT to create a virtual personal shopping experience, offering users curated collections of clothing and accessories tailored to their style preferences, budget, and specific needs. By offering a personalized and convenient shopping experience, startups can enhance user satisfaction and drive sales.

8. Community engagement and user-generated content: Leverage ChatGPT to foster a vibrant fashion community where users can share their style tips, outfit inspiration, and fashion finds. The AI-powered chatbot can facilitate discussions, answer questions, and encourage users to engage with one another, creating a supportive and inclusive space for fashion enthusiasts.

By leveraging ChatGPT in AI-driven fashion and style advice services, startups can offer users personalized, engaging, and on-trend guidance, helping them cultivate their personal style and make confident wardrobe choices. This not only enhances user satisfaction but also contributes to the overall success and growth of the startup in the competitive fashion and style advice market.

Chapter 44: AI-Driven Interior Design Solutions Leveraging ChatGPT

In this chapter, we will explore the potential of ChatGPT in revolutionizing the interior design industry by offering AI-driven interior design solutions. By harnessing the power of ChatGPT, startups can develop innovative platforms that cater to the diverse needs of users, helping them create beautiful, functional, and personalized living spaces.

1. Personalized design recommendations: Utilize ChatGPT to generate personalized interior design recommendations based on users' style preferences, room dimensions, and functional requirements. By offering tailored suggestions, startups can help users discover new design ideas, furniture, and décor that align with their unique tastes and needs.

2. Virtual room planning and layout optimization: Leverage ChatGPT to create a virtual room planning and layout optimization platform that allows users to upload images or blueprints of their existing spaces, receive layout suggestions, and visualize different design options. The AI-powered chatbot can offer guidance on furniture placement, traffic flow, and space utilization, helping users create functional and visually appealing interiors.

3. AI-generated design mood boards and style guides: Integrate ChatGPT into your interior design platform to create AI-generated design mood boards and style guides tailored to users' specific interests and preferences. By offering targeted inspiration and guidance, startups can help users visualize their dream spaces and make informed design decisions.

4. Color and material suggestions: Utilize ChatGPT to provide

users with personalized color and material suggestions for their interiors, taking into account factors such as lighting, room size, and existing furnishings. By offering practical and creative options, startups can help users create harmonious and aesthetically pleasing living spaces.

5. Budget optimization and shopping assistance: Leverage ChatGPT to develop a budget optimization and shopping assistance system that helps users find the perfect furnishings and décor within their budget. The AI-driven chatbot can offer guidance on cost-saving strategies, suggest budget-friendly alternatives, and provide insights into the best places to shop for interior design items.

6. Sustainable and eco-friendly design: Integrate ChatGPT into your interior design platform to provide users with guidance on sustainable and eco-friendly design choices, including environmentally responsible materials, energy-efficient lighting, and waste reduction strategies. By promoting sustainable practices, startups can contribute to a more environmentally responsible interior design industry.

7. DIY and upcycling ideas: Utilize ChatGPT to offer users creative DIY and upcycling ideas, helping them transform their existing furniture and décor items into new and unique pieces. By encouraging resourcefulness and creativity, startups can foster a sense of personal accomplishment and pride in users' interior design projects.

8. Community engagement and user-generated content: Leverage ChatGPT to create a vibrant interior design community where users can share their design tips, project inspiration, and personal experiences. The AI-powered chatbot can facilitate discussions, answer questions, and encourage users to engage with one another, creating a supportive and inclusive space for design enthusiasts.

By leveraging ChatGPT in AI-driven interior design solutions, startups can offer users personalized, engaging, and practical guidance, helping them create beautiful, functional, and personalized living spaces. This not only enhances user satisfaction but also contributes to the overall success and growth of the startup in the competitive interior design market.

Chapter 45: ChatGPT-Powered Art and Design Services

In this chapter, we will delve into the potential of ChatGPT in revolutionizing the art and design industry by offering AI-driven art and design services. By harnessing the power of ChatGPT, startups can develop innovative platforms that cater to a diverse range of creative needs, helping artists, designers, and clients collaborate effectively and produce stunning visual content.

1. AI-generated design concepts: Utilize ChatGPT to generate unique design concepts based on users' creative briefs, requirements, and preferences. By offering a wide range of AI-driven ideas, startups can help users explore new creative directions and jumpstart their design process.

2. Art and design feedback: Leverage ChatGPT to provide users with constructive feedback on their art and design projects. The AI-powered chatbot can analyze users' work and offer suggestions for improvement, helping them refine their skills and produce high-quality visual content.

3. Creative collaboration: Integrate ChatGPT into your art and design platform to facilitate collaboration between artists, designers, and clients. The AI-driven chatbot can help users communicate their ideas effectively, provide real-time feedback, and negotiate project requirements, resulting in a smooth and efficient creative process.

4. AI-generated visual content: Utilize ChatGPT to create AI-generated visual content, such as graphic design elements, illustrations, and digital art. By offering a range of unique and customizable visuals, startups can help users save time and resources while producing visually engaging content.

5. Design education and tutorials: Leverage ChatGPT to offer users educational resources and tutorials on various design techniques, software, and tools. The AI-powered chatbot can provide step-by-step guidance, answer questions, and help users enhance their design skills and knowledge.

6. Art and design curation: Integrate ChatGPT into your art and design platform to curate personalized collections of art and design work based on users' preferences and interests. By offering tailored recommendations, startups can help users discover new artists, styles, and trends.

7. Copyright and intellectual property guidance: Utilize ChatGPT to provide users with guidance on copyright and intellectual property matters related to their art and design projects. The AI-driven chatbot can help users navigate complex legal issues, ensuring that their work is protected and compliant with relevant regulations.

8. Community engagement and networking: Leverage ChatGPT to create a vibrant art and design community where users can share their work, seek feedback, and connect with like-minded individuals. The AI-powered chatbot can facilitate discussions, answer questions, and foster a sense of connection and support among users.

By leveraging ChatGPT in AI-driven art and design services, startups can offer users personalized, engaging, and practical guidance, helping them produce stunning visual content while fostering collaboration and creative growth. This not only enhances user satisfaction but also contributes to the overall success and growth of the startup in the competitive art and design market.

Chapter 46: ChatGPT-Powered Healthcare and Medical Services

In this chapter, we will discuss the potential of ChatGPT in revolutionizing healthcare and medical services by offering AI-driven solutions. By leveraging ChatGPT, startups can develop innovative platforms that cater to a diverse range of healthcare needs, helping patients, medical professionals, and healthcare providers access information, communicate effectively, and make informed decisions.

1. Symptom checker and preliminary diagnosis: Utilize ChatGPT to create an AI-powered symptom checker and preliminary diagnosis tool that helps users understand their symptoms and potential medical conditions. By offering accurate and accessible information, startups can help users make informed decisions about seeking medical care and managing their health.

2. Medical information and resources: Leverage ChatGPT to provide users with reliable medical information and resources on a wide range of topics, including medications, treatment options, and preventive care. The AI-powered chatbot can offer personalized and evidence-based guidance, helping users navigate complex medical information.

3. Healthcare provider search and recommendations: Integrate ChatGPT into your healthcare platform to help users find and select healthcare providers based on their preferences, location, and insurance coverage. By offering tailored suggestions, startups can help users access quality healthcare services that suit their unique needs.

4. Virtual health consultations: Utilize ChatGPT to create a virtual health consultation platform that connects users with

medical professionals for real-time advice and support. The AI-driven chatbot can facilitate communication, triage patient concerns, and help medical professionals provide personalized care.

5. Medication management and adherence: Leverage ChatGPT to develop a medication management and adherence tool that helps users track their medications, understand potential side effects, and receive reminders for optimal adherence. By offering practical support, startups can help users manage their medications effectively and improve their overall health outcomes.

6. Mental health support: Integrate ChatGPT into your healthcare platform to provide users with mental health support and resources, including self-help strategies, stress management techniques, and crisis intervention services. By offering accessible and empathetic support, startups can contribute to improved mental health and well-being for users.

7. Patient communication and support: Utilize ChatGPT to facilitate communication between patients, caregivers, and medical professionals, helping users access support, coordinate care, and share important medical information. The AI-powered chatbot can help users navigate the healthcare system and foster a sense of connection and understanding among all parties involved.

8. Medical research and data analysis: Leverage ChatGPT to analyze medical research and data, helping healthcare providers and researchers identify trends, patterns, and insights that can inform clinical practice and drive innovation in healthcare.

By leveraging ChatGPT in AI-driven healthcare and medical services, startups can offer users personalized, engaging, and practical guidance, helping them access information, communicate effectively, and make informed decisions about their health. This not only enhances user satisfaction but also contributes to the overall success and growth of the startup in the competitive healthcare market.

Chapter 47: AI-Driven Music and Sound Design Leveraging ChatGPT

In this chapter, we will explore the potential of ChatGPT in revolutionizing the music and sound design industry by offering AI-driven solutions. By harnessing the power of ChatGPT, startups can develop innovative platforms that cater to a diverse range of creative needs, helping musicians, composers, sound designers, and clients collaborate effectively and produce captivating audio content.

1. AI-generated music and soundscapes: Utilize ChatGPT to create AI-generated music and soundscapes based on users' creative briefs, requirements, and preferences. By offering a wide range of AI-driven compositions, startups can help users explore new creative directions and jumpstart their music and sound design projects.

2. Music and sound design feedback: Leverage ChatGPT to provide users with constructive feedback on their music and sound design projects. The AI-powered chatbot can analyze users' work and offer suggestions for improvement, helping them refine their skills and produce high-quality audio content.

3. Creative collaboration: Integrate ChatGPT into your music and sound design platform to facilitate collaboration between musicians, composers, sound designers, and clients. The AI-driven chatbot can help users communicate their ideas effectively, provide real-time feedback, and negotiate project requirements, resulting in a smooth and efficient creative process.

4. AI-generated sample libraries: Utilize ChatGPT to create AI-generated sample libraries that offer a diverse range of unique

and customizable sounds, loops, and effects. By offering a wide array of audio resources, startups can help users save time and resources while producing captivating audio content.

5. Music and sound design education and tutorials: Leverage ChatGPT to offer users educational resources and tutorials on various music production techniques, software, and tools. The AI-powered chatbot can provide step-by-step guidance, answer questions, and help users enhance their music and sound design skills and knowledge.

6. Music and sound design curation: Integrate ChatGPT into your music and sound design platform to curate personalized collections of music and sound design work based on users' preferences and interests. By offering tailored recommendations, startups can help users discover new artists, styles, and trends.

7. Copyright and intellectual property guidance: Utilize ChatGPT to provide users with guidance on copyright and intellectual property matters related to their music and sound design projects. The AI-driven chatbot can help users navigate complex legal issues, ensuring that their work is protected and compliant with relevant regulations.

8. Community engagement and networking: Leverage ChatGPT to create a vibrant music and sound design community where users can share their work, seek feedback, and connect with like-minded individuals. The AI-powered chatbot can facilitate discussions, answer questions, and foster a sense of connection and support among users.

By leveraging ChatGPT in AI-driven music and sound design services, startups can offer users personalized, engaging, and practical guidance, helping them produce captivating audio content while fostering collaboration and creative growth. This not only enhances user satisfaction but also contributes to the overall success and growth of the startup in the competitive music and sound design market.

Chapter 48: ChatGPT-Powered Literary Analysis and Reviews

In this chapter, we will explore the potential of ChatGPT in transforming the landscape of literary analysis and reviews. By harnessing the power of ChatGPT, startups can develop innovative platforms that cater to a diverse range of literary enthusiasts, helping readers, authors, publishers, and critics collaborate effectively and engage with literature in a new, AI-driven way.

1. AI-generated literary analysis: Utilize ChatGPT to generate literary analysis for various works of literature, including novels, poems, plays, and essays. The AI-powered analysis can delve into aspects like themes, symbolism, character development, and writing style, offering readers a comprehensive understanding of the literary work.

2. Personalized reading recommendations: Leverage ChatGPT to curate personalized reading recommendations for users based on their preferences, reading history, and interests. By offering tailored suggestions, startups can help users discover new authors, genres, and literary works that cater to their tastes.

3. Book reviews and summaries: Integrate ChatGPT into your literary platform to generate book reviews and summaries that provide users with a concise overview of the work's content, quality, and relevance. The AI-driven reviews can help users make informed decisions about which books to read and engage with.

4. Author support and feedback: Utilize ChatGPT to provide authors with constructive feedback on their literary works, helping them improve their writing and storytelling skills.

The AI-powered chatbot can offer suggestions for revisions, edits, and enhancements, enabling authors to produce high-quality content.

5. Creative writing assistance: Leverage ChatGPT to offer users creative writing assistance, including story ideas, character development, and plot structure. The AI-driven chatbot can provide guidance and inspiration, helping users enhance their writing skills and bring their stories to life.

6. Literary discussions and book clubs: Integrate ChatGPT into your literary platform to facilitate discussions and book clubs, allowing users to engage with other like-minded readers, share insights, and explore literature in a social setting. The AI-powered chatbot can moderate discussions, pose thought-provoking questions, and foster a sense of community among users.

7. Literary education and tutorials: Utilize ChatGPT to offer users educational resources and tutorials on various literary techniques, styles, and historical contexts. The AI-powered chatbot can provide step-by-step guidance, answer questions, and help users deepen their understanding and appreciation of literature.

8. Publishing industry insights: Leverage ChatGPT to provide users with insights into the publishing industry, including trends, opportunities, and challenges. The AI-driven chatbot can help aspiring authors navigate the complexities of the publishing process, increasing their chances of success and visibility in the literary world.

By leveraging ChatGPT in AI-driven literary analysis and reviews, startups can offer users personalized, engaging, and practical guidance, helping them engage with literature in a more profound and meaningful way. This not only enhances user satisfaction but also contributes to the overall success and growth of the startup in the competitive literary market.

Chapter 49: AI-Driven Personal Finance Management Leveraging ChatGPT

In this chapter, we will discuss the potential of ChatGPT in revolutionizing personal finance management by offering AI-driven solutions. By leveraging ChatGPT, startups can develop innovative platforms that cater to a diverse range of financial needs, helping users make informed decisions, manage their finances effectively, and achieve their financial goals.

1. Budgeting and expense tracking: Utilize ChatGPT to create AI-powered budgeting and expense tracking tools that help users monitor their spending, identify patterns, and make adjustments as needed. By offering personalized and actionable insights, startups can assist users in maintaining control over their finances and staying on track with their financial goals.

2. Financial goal setting and planning: Leverage ChatGPT to help users establish and prioritize financial goals, such as saving for retirement, buying a home, or paying off debt. The AI-driven chatbot can provide guidance on setting realistic goals, developing a plan, and adjusting strategies as circumstances change.

3. Investment advice and portfolio management: Integrate ChatGPT into your personal finance platform to offer AI-driven investment advice and portfolio management services. By analyzing users' financial goals, risk tolerance, and investment preferences, the AI-powered chatbot can recommend tailored investment strategies and monitor portfolio performance.

4. Debt management and repayment strategies: Utilize

ChatGPT to provide users with personalized debt management and repayment strategies, taking into account their unique financial situations and goals. The AI-driven chatbot can offer guidance on consolidating debt, negotiating with creditors, and prioritizing payments to minimize interest costs and expedite debt repayment.

5. Tax planning and filing assistance: Leverage ChatGPT to offer users tax planning and filing assistance, helping them navigate complex tax regulations, identify deductions and credits, and ensure compliance with tax laws. By offering practical support, startups can help users minimize their tax liabilities and avoid potential penalties.

6. Financial education and resources: Integrate ChatGPT into your personal finance platform to provide users with educational resources on various financial topics, such as investing, credit management, insurance, and retirement planning. The AI-powered chatbot can answer questions, provide step-by-step guidance, and help users enhance their financial knowledge and decision-making skills.

7. Savings and account optimization: Utilize ChatGPT to analyze users' financial accounts, such as checking, savings, and investment accounts, and recommend strategies for optimizing returns, minimizing fees, and maximizing account benefits. By offering personalized advice, startups can help users make the most of their financial resources.

8. Financial alerts and reminders: Leverage ChatGPT to send users timely financial alerts and reminders, such as upcoming bill payments, investment opportunities, or changes in interest rates. By keeping users informed and engaged, startups can help them stay on top of their finances and avoid potential pitfalls.

By leveraging ChatGPT in AI-driven personal finance management, startups can offer users personalized, engaging, and practical guidance, helping them manage their finances effectively and achieve their financial goals. This not only enhances user satisfaction but also contributes to the overall success and growth of the startup in the competitive personal finance market.

Chapter 50: Leveraging ChatGPT to Drive Profits in the Automotive Industry for Startups

In this chapter, we will delve into the potential of ChatGPT in revolutionizing the automotive industry by offering AI-driven solutions. By harnessing the power of ChatGPT, startups can develop innovative platforms and services that cater to a diverse range of automotive needs, helping customers, manufacturers, and dealers effectively engage with the automotive ecosystem and drive profits.

1. AI-driven automotive sales assistance: Utilize ChatGPT to create AI-powered chatbots that assist potential customers in the car-buying process. These chatbots can provide personalized vehicle recommendations based on customers' preferences, budget, and requirements, guiding them through the entire purchasing process and answering any questions they might have.

2. Virtual showrooms and product demonstrations: Leverage ChatGPT to develop virtual showrooms and AI-driven product demonstrations that showcase vehicle features, specifications, and performance in an engaging and immersive manner. By offering customers a virtual experience, startups can help automotive manufacturers and dealers generate leads and increase sales.

3. AI-powered vehicle maintenance and diagnostics: Integrate ChatGPT into your automotive platform to offer AI-driven vehicle maintenance and diagnostics services. The AI-powered chatbot can help customers identify potential issues with their vehicles, suggest maintenance tasks, and recommend nearby service centers, enhancing customer

satisfaction and generating revenue for service providers.

4. Personalized aftermarket services and accessories: Utilize ChatGPT to recommend personalized aftermarket services and accessories to customers based on their vehicle's make, model, and preferences. By offering tailored suggestions, startups can drive sales for automotive service providers and accessory manufacturers.

5. AI-driven automotive financing and insurance: Leverage ChatGPT to offer AI-driven financing and insurance options to customers, helping them navigate complex financial products and find the most suitable solutions for their needs. By offering personalized guidance and support, startups can generate revenue through partnerships with financial institutions and insurance providers.

6. Automotive education and resources: Integrate ChatGPT into your automotive platform to provide users with educational resources on various automotive topics, such as vehicle maintenance, fuel efficiency, and driving safety. The AI-powered chatbot can answer questions, provide step-by-step guidance, and help users enhance their automotive knowledge and skills.

7. Fleet management and logistics: Utilize ChatGPT to develop AI-driven solutions for fleet management and logistics, assisting businesses in optimizing vehicle usage, route planning, and fuel consumption. By offering advanced analytics and insights, startups can help businesses reduce costs and improve operational efficiency.

8. AI-powered automotive marketing: Leverage ChatGPT to create targeted and personalized automotive marketing campaigns for manufacturers and dealers, analyzing customer preferences, demographics, and behavior to deliver relevant and engaging content. By offering AI-driven marketing

solutions, startups can help businesses increase brand visibility, generate leads, and boost sales.

By leveraging ChatGPT in the automotive industry, startups can offer personalized, engaging, and practical solutions, helping customers, manufacturers, and dealers effectively engage with the automotive ecosystem and drive profits. This not only enhances user satisfaction but also contributes to the overall success and growth of the startup in the competitive automotive market.

Chapter 51: Leveraging ChatGPT to Fuel Innovation in the Oil and Gas Industry for Startups

In this chapter, we will explore the potential of ChatGPT in revolutionizing the oil and gas industry by offering AI-driven solutions. By harnessing the power of ChatGPT, startups can develop innovative platforms and services that cater to a diverse range of oil and gas industry needs, helping businesses optimize operations, reduce costs, and enhance safety.

1. AI-driven asset management and maintenance: Utilize ChatGPT to create AI-powered asset management and maintenance solutions that help oil and gas companies monitor equipment performance, predict potential issues, and schedule maintenance tasks. By offering advanced analytics and insights, startups can assist businesses in reducing downtime, minimizing costs, and prolonging asset life.

2. AI-powered exploration and drilling: Leverage ChatGPT to develop AI-driven solutions for oil and gas exploration and drilling, assisting businesses in identifying potential reserves, optimizing drilling strategies, and managing risks. By offering advanced data analysis and decision-making support, startups can help businesses increase efficiency and maximize resource recovery.

3. AI-driven supply chain and logistics optimization: Integrate ChatGPT into your oil and gas platform to offer AI-driven supply chain and logistics optimization solutions, helping businesses streamline transportation, storage, and distribution of oil and gas products. By providing advanced

analytics and real-time visibility, startups can help businesses reduce costs, improve operational efficiency, and enhance customer satisfaction.

4. AI-powered safety and risk management: Utilize ChatGPT to develop AI-driven safety and risk management solutions for the oil and gas industry, helping businesses identify potential hazards, assess risks, and implement mitigation strategies. By offering proactive and data-driven safety solutions, startups can help businesses protect their workforce, assets, and reputation.

5. AI-driven regulatory compliance and reporting: Leverage ChatGPT to offer AI-driven regulatory compliance and reporting solutions for the oil and gas industry, assisting businesses in navigating complex regulations, tracking compliance, and generating reports. By offering practical guidance and support, startups can help businesses minimize the risk of fines, penalties, and reputational damage.

6. AI-powered energy trading and market analysis: Integrate ChatGPT into your oil and gas platform to provide AI-driven energy trading and market analysis solutions, helping businesses optimize trading strategies, forecast price movements, and identify opportunities. By offering advanced analytics and decision-making support, startups can help businesses maximize profits and minimize risks.

7. Workforce training and development: Utilize ChatGPT to offer AI-driven workforce training and development solutions for the oil and gas industry, providing employees with interactive learning experiences, tailored content, and real-time feedback. By offering personalized and engaging training solutions, startups can help businesses enhance workforce skills, productivity, and retention.

8. AI-powered environmental monitoring and sustainability:

Leverage ChatGPT to develop AI-driven environmental monitoring and sustainability solutions for the oil and gas industry, helping businesses track emissions, optimize resource use, and implement sustainable practices. By offering data-driven insights and support, startups can help businesses minimize their environmental impact and meet sustainability targets.

By leveraging ChatGPT in the oil and gas industry, startups can offer personalized, engaging, and practical solutions, helping businesses optimize operations, reduce costs, and enhance safety. This not only enhances user satisfaction but also contributes to the overall success and growth of the startup in the competitive oil and gas market.

Don't miss out!

Visit the website below and you can sign up to receive emails whenever David Murray-Hundley publishes a new book. There's no charge and no obligation.

https://books2read.com/r/B-A-SFKY-FOYIC

About the Author

David Murray-Hundley, fondly known as "The Grumpy Entrepreneur," is a remarkably distinguished figure in the world of entrepreneurship and business. Renowned for his straight-talking, no-nonsense attitude, and an unshakeable resolve, he has created a reputation that reflects both his business acumen and his unique persona.

Born in the United Kingdom, Murray-Hundley began his career in the technology sector, where he quickly made his mark. His first venture was Commerce One, a successful tech startup that he co-founded in the late 90s. Despite its initial success, the company was a casualty of the dot com crash, which served as a pivotal learning experience for Murray-Hundley.

Read more at https://www.parioventures.com.

About the Publisher

9 7 9 8 2 2 3 7 1 2 4 5 9